# Samuel Cunard
## Pioneer of the Atlantic Steamship

"Ouvrage publié à l'occasion du Centenaire de la Confédération Canadienne, grâce à une subvention de la Commission du Centenaire".

"Published on the occasion of the Centennial of Canadian Confederation and subsidized by the Centennial Commission".

Sir Samuel Cunard, from a lithograph done circa 1840, when he was fifty-three years of age.

# Samuel Cunard

## Pioneer of the Atlantic Steamship

by KAY GRANT

Illustrated with photographs

### Abelard-Schuman

LONDON   NEW YORK   TORONTO

| London | New York | Toronto |
|--------|----------|---------|
| Abelard-Schuman | Abelard-Schuman | Abelard-Schuman |
| Limited | Limited | Canada Limited |
| 8 King St. WC2 | 6 West 57th St. | 896 Queen St. W. |

Printed in the United States of America

DESIGN BY Stanley S. Drate

# Acknowledgments

There are many descendants of Sir Samuel Cunard living today in the United States, Canada, England and continental Europe. I have been fortunate enough to meet a few of them, to correspond with others, and to examine family papers and letters. I wish to thank, in particular, Sir Henry Cunard, Miss Laura Cunard, Mrs. Robert Harcourt, Mrs. John Barrington, Mrs. Nigel Dugdale and her family, Mrs. John Charrington, Mrs. George Loveday, Mrs. O. Story.

The files of the Provincial Archives of Nova Scotia, the New Brunswick Museum and the University of New Brunswick Library furnished some material about the early Cunards, about life in the Atlantic colonies during the early years of the nineteenth century and about local ships and shipping. I am grateful also to many individuals in the maritime provinces who furnished valuable records, particularly to Rev. Robert Coote and Canon Bradshaw, both of Nova Scotia; Mrs. Spicer of the York-Sunbury Historical Association in New Brunswick; and Dr. Louise Manny of Newcastle, New Brunswick, who is the supreme

( 5 )

authority on Sir Samuel's dashing brother Joseph Cunard. Mr. D. O. Pam of the Edmonton Historical Society furnished information about Bush Hill House near London. Mr. Miller of the Twickenham Reference Library gave information about the Haliburton and Cunard houses in that part of suburban London.

Special thanks are due to the Cunard Steam-Ship Company, which placed all its records at my disposal and allowed me to compare at first hand the fabulous queens of the ocean with the written description of the first small ships of the line.

—K. G.

## PICTURE CREDITS

The Public Archives of Canada: Frontispiece, pp. 28, 38, 40, 42, 73, 167, 170, 187
Cunard Line Limited: pp. 95, 97, 110, 145, 181, 184
Jean Morton: p. 103
Nova Scotia Information Service: pp. 133, 135
Mr. D. O. Pam, Edmonton Reference Library: p. 149
Province of Nova Scotia Archives, Halifax: p. 157
Dr. Louise Manny: p. 172

The photograph on the back of the jacket, courtesy of The Cunard Steam-Ship Company Ltd., shows a scale model of the Q4, the $85-million Cunard superliner now under construction.

# Illustrations

The *Shannon* and the *Chesapeake* entering Halifax harbor, 1813   28
George Ramsay, Earl of Dalhousie   38
William Edward Parry   40
The *Accommodation*   42
The first flag of the Cunard fleet   49
The *Royal William*   73
Robert Napier   95
George Burns   97
The *Samson*   103
Flag of the first Cunard steamship, 1840   106
The *Britannia*   110
Thomas Chandler Haliburton   133
Joseph Howe   135
A ship of Cunard's Mediterranean fleet, 1851   145
Bush Hill House   149
The Cunard coat of arms   156
Portrait of Sir Samuel Cunard   157
Enos Collins   167
Laura Haliburton Cunard   170

( 7 )

Joseph Cunard, circa 1864   172
Cunard house flag of 1878–1934   179
The *Lusitania*   181
The *Mauretania*   181
The *Queen Mary*   184
The *Queen Elizabeth*   184
Cunard–White Star house flag   187

## CHILDREN AND GRANDCHILDREN
### OF SAMUEL CUNARD AND SUSAN DUFFUS

*EDWARD,* b. Dec. 31, 1815
m. Mary Bache Mc-Evers, May, 1849

xSamuel
Bache Edward
Mary
Edward
Gordon
Jeanette
Anne
Caroline Margaret

*MARY,* b. Apr. 21, 1817
m. James Horse-field Peters, Sept. 1837

xSusan Margaret
Mary Caroline
Thomas Sherman
Frederick
Anthony
Margaret Laura

x*SUSAN,* b. Feb. 6, 1819

*MARGARET ANN,* b. Mar. 14, 1820
m. William Leigh Mellish, Oct. 1843

Edward Leigh
Agnes
xWilliam Chambers
Henry
Evelyn
George

*SARAH JANE (JANE),* b. Dec. 21, 1821
m. Gilbert William Francklyn, Sept. 1840

Margaret Moore
Charles Gilbert
Gwladys Elizabeth
George Edward
Frances Mary
Annie Kate
Laura Isabel
Helen Jane
Edith

*ANNE ELIZABETH (ANN)*
  b. Mar. 25, 1823
m. Ralph Shuttleworth Allen,
  Sept. 1844

Ralph Edward
George Cunard
Fanny Mary
Henry
Philip

*WILLIAM*, b. Apr. 9, 1825
m. Laura Charlotte Haliburton,
  Dec. 1851

xLouisa Neville
 Alice Mary
 William Samuel
xArthur   ⎱
xHerbert  ⎰ twins
 Ernest Haliburton
 Cyril Grant

*ISABELLA (ISABEL)* b. Feb.
  4, 1827
m. Henry Holden, Oct. 1850

Harry
Maude
Blanche
Ethel

*ELIZABETH*, b. Jan. 22, 1828
unmarried

x Died in infancy or early childhood.

# 1

The steamboat had been in general use on canals and rivers for almost thirty years before anyone dared to trust it on the open ocean. "One might as well talk of making a voyage to the moon," the scientists warned, "as to talk about crossing the Atlantic in a steamer." Samuel Cunard, the man who founded the steamship line that still bears his name, was one of the pioneers who challenged this statement. He started the first regularly scheduled steamship service between England and America.

Cunard revolutionized ocean transportation and made a giant contribution to world development. As other shipowners followed his example, and as stories about the speed and comfort of the new ocean steamers reached the crowded cities of the old world, more and more people began to dream of emigrating to new lands, of exploring new continents. The rapid growth of the United States, from a population of about 20 million in 1840 to almost 150 million a hundred years later, would not have been possible without the ocean steamer, which was also responsible for the great nineteenth-century expansion of the British Empire.

Samuel Cunard's ancestors were Dutch Quakers who came to America in 1683. They settled near the Delaware River, in the new region called Pennsylvania, and began to clear the land.

One day, according to a family legend, Thomas Cunard and his sons were tilling a field when their plow turned up a bag of gold coins—some pirate's loot, they assumed, for in those days the Atlantic coast was swarming with pirates, who hid in the bays and rivers when pursued and buried their stolen treasure. The lucky find enabled Thomas and his sons to buy a ship at nearby Philadelphia. This was the beginning of a shipping business that prospered for almost a hundred years.

When the American Revolution began in 1775, Thomas Cunard's descendants were among the rich and respected first families of Philadelphia. The shipping business founded by Thomas was in the hands of Robert Cunard and his son Abraham. Their fleet of vessels carried trade goods to and from England, the West Indies, and the coastal towns of the thirteen colonies.

But Robert Cunard was a loyalist, a British supporter. When the Revolution was over and the expulsion of the loyalists began, everything he owned was confiscated— his home, his property, his business. He was convicted of treason and banished from the new United States of America. With his sons and daughters, he fled to the British colonies north of New England.

In all, fifty thousand loyalists were evacuated to the

British colonies. Two-thirds of them settled in the Atlantic provinces of Nova Scotia and New Brunswick. The British government, well aware of the value of these well-educated pioneers, spent more than a million pounds to help them in getting established. The refugees were given food, clothing, free land and lumber to build houses. Hundreds of jobs were created for them.

The Cunard family sailed from New York in the spring of 1783, exactly one hundred years after their ancestors had settled in Pennsylvania. Their small ship, one of a convoy of twenty, carried almost two hundred passengers, among them Thomas Murphy of Charleston, South Carolina, a shipbuilder who in pre-Revolutionary days had built traders for the Cunard fleet.

Before the voyage ended, Abraham Cunard had fallen in love with Thomas Murphy's daughter Margaret, a tall, spirited girl with dark eyes, who had somehow reached the age of twenty-five without finding a husband. Abraham was a quiet, scholarly man of twenty-seven, not quite as tall as Margaret.

The refugees were put ashore near the mouth of the Saint John River in New Brunswick, where British officials were waiting to greet them and help them to select their future homes. Robert Cunard was given a grant of land near Saint John. Thomas Murphy, who had brought along many slaves and field hands as part of his household, chose a large uncleared tract in a new settlement called Rawdon in Nova Scotia. Some British soldiers who had fought under Lord Rawdon in South Carolina had already settled there and had given the place its name. Abraham Cunard decided to strike out on his own and try his luck in Halifax, the chief seaport on the rocky Atlantic shore of Nova Scotia.

At that time, Nova Scotia was a wilderness with a few scattered settlements, mostly along the seacoast. Halifax, the only town, had been built to provide a base of operations for British attacks against the French in Canada. The site had been selected, the trees cut down, streets laid out in precise squares and houses built, all in one year—1749. Behind the town a fortified mound, called Citadel Hill, served as a lookout.

When the Revolution began, Halifax became, overnight, the most important naval and military base in British North America, the only seaport on the Atlantic where British warships could be refitted and where supplies and ammunition could be stored. Ships of the Royal Navy shuttled in and out of the harbor. The streets were filled with marching Redcoats. By the time Abraham arrived, the once quiet settlement had become a crowded bustling place, spreading out in all directions as more and more loyalists poured in.

Long before the Revolution ended, Abraham had realized that if the colonies won their fight for freedom, his father's business would be confiscated, and the rich, smooth life his family had known would end. With characteristic thoroughness, he had prepared himself for exile. He knew that the Atlantic provinces were undeveloped, covered with forest. The loyalists would have to clear land and build houses. So Abraham, who loved books and music, took up carpentry and became proficient in that trade.

In Halifax, his skill as a carpenter and his knowledge of ships and timber got him a job as a foreman artificer with the Royal Engineers in the government lumberyard, an important department in the days when wood was the only material used in shipbuilding. At the lumberyard, masts and spars and squared timber, rafted down from the King's Woods, were trimmed to size for use in the shipyards, and in various departments of the army and navy.

Given a choice of land in several locations, Abraham chose a shore lot in the undeveloped area between the town and the naval station, a narrow strip of about ten acres running steeply uphill from the waterfront to a muddy lane that was later named Brunswick Street. It was a wise choice. As Halifax expanded, the value of the land skyrocketed, and more ships crowded the waterfront.

Near the top of the hill, he built a modest two-story house of squared timber with a gambrel roof and a gable end facing the water. Abraham designed the house himself and built most of it with his own hands. He made furniture of thick pine planks. When everything was finished, he rode forty miles through the woods to the Murphy home at Rawdon. There he and Margaret were married.

All her life, Margaret had been accustomed to luxury. She had been sheltered and waited on. In Halifax she had one servant—an African slave who had grown up in her father's household—to do the hard work of carrying water from the town pump, milking the indispensable cow, tending the garden, and chopping firewood. For many loyalists, used to gentle living, the time of adjustment to pioneer life was hard and bitter. Margaret managed better than most. She had some help, at least, and the house Abraham built was warm in winter.

Like all colonial outposts, Halifax had its coterie of government officials sent out from England. The commander-in-chief of the colonial armed forces was stationed there. The naval base, with an admiral in command, was headquarters for all the British North American fleet, including Bermuda and the West Indies.

Social etiquette was rigid, and class distinctions were stringently observed. A loyalist might live in a log cabin, but if he had been well connected in the American colonies, he was accepted as a member of upper-class society. This included the governor and his aides, the Anglican bishop, officers of the garrison and the fleet and some, but not all, of the rich merchants. New-rich merchants without the proper education and background were excluded from the balls and bacchanalian dinners at which the ladies wore silks and velvets and the officers appeared in full-dress uniform, complete with swords and powdered wigs.

Abraham and his wife were received, as they had expected to be, into this provincial imitation of London society. Margaret unpacked her best gown and her husband's satin knee breeches and silk stockings, and the two went off to dine with the governor and his lady. The official residence was not much more opulent than the Cunards' small cottage.

The wellborn loyalists were extremely class-conscious, which was not surprising, considering that they had given up their homes rather than accept the democratic ideals of the new republic of the United States.

In the prosperous years following the Revolution, while Halifax grew in size and importance, both as a defense outpost and as a distributing point for trade goods from Britain and the West Indies, many of the loyalists grew rich overnight. Abraham was not one of them, though he was moderately successful. A sober, thrifty man, respected by everyone, he stuck to his job at the lumberyard and in time rose to a position of some importance. With a staff of assistants, he handled all the requisitions for trimmed lumber. Specifications for any government building project, including ships, had to be submitted to his department.

To supplement his income, he designed a few houses and hired a crew of workmen to build them, although he continued to do much of the fine carpentry work himself, after hours. He put up such a handsome home for Governor Wentworth's secretary that orders came in for more like it. When his family outgrew the small settler's cottage, Abraham built a bigger one on the same lot. The record of one odd job, which he completed in 1792, stands in the records of St. Paul's Anglican Church as "an alteration in the pews of the middle aisle." Abraham and Margaret belonged to this church.

Always aware of the growing value of real estate, he bought another piece of land along Brunswick Street, which for the time being provided pasture for the family cow.

Abraham and Margaret had nine children, two girls and seven boys. The first child, Mary, was born in 1784. The second child, Samuel, who was never called anything but Sam until he acquired a title seventy-two years later, was born on November 21, 1787. William, Susan, Edward, Joseph, John, Thomas and Henry followed in that order.

Sam had a happy childhood. All the children were devoted to their mother, who was more demonstrative and changeable than their quiet father. Abraham never seemed to doubt that his oldest son would grow up to be a success, because Sam resembled his grandfather, Robert Cunard, who in the old Philadelphia days had been considered a very sharp businessman.

Sam was an alert, inquisitive little boy with wide-awake brown eyes. Ships were his great love. From the time he could sit up and look out of a window, he watched them coming and going—square-rigged merchantmen from the sugar islands, fishing schooners from the Banks, coasters from the outports, traders from New England, sometimes a privateer with a captured French ship. All the bustle and romance of a busy port was spread out before him, just down the hill from his father's house. It was a picture he never tired of looking at, even when he was an old man and had seen the great cities of the world.

A small shallop ferried passengers across the mile-wide harbor to Dartmouth. At intervals during the day, the ferryman could be heard at the slip, alternately blowing on a conch shell and crying "Over! Over!" until the shallop was filled. Farther out, frigates and cruisers of the Royal Navy rode at anchor. And towering over everything was the giant hoisting tackle at the careening yard where ships were "hove down," or pulled over on their sides, for repairs.

Once a month, from April through November, the packet docked at the King's Wharf with the English mail. Packets were ten-gun brigs, commanded by officers of the Royal Navy. They ran between Falmouth on the south coast of England and New York, with a stopover at Halifax coming and going. All the mail for British North America was put ashore at Halifax and redistributed from there.

The arrival of the Royal Mail was a great occasion. The whole town went down to the waterfront to greet the incoming vessel and hear the latest news from England. Sam usually managed to be there in time to watch the mail come ashore. The two or three letterbags were slung on an oar carried shoulder-high by two sailors, and delivered with solemn ceremony to the post office. An officer in a cocked hat and full uniform, his pistol at the ready, marched alongside.

At the wharves, where the traders brought their cargoes, the ships were berthed so close together that their ranked bowsprits made a canopy over the warehouses and drying sheds. There was a smell of hemp and tar and fish and spices. The waterfront was a dangerous place for young boys to play, because the sailors often celebrated their return to port by getting drunk and fighting among themselves. But Sam and his friends slipped away to the docks whenever they could. They watched the dark West Indians—dressed like pirates, with gold hoops in their ears, and scarlet cummerbunds—unloading barrels of rum and molasses from the traders. They listened to stories told by old sailors who sat around splicing rope and patching sails. And like all boys who live beside the sea, they dreamed of shipping out on a heeling windjammer, to see those faraway places the sailors talked about.

One of Sam's earliest recollections was of a sunny morning, a time his father always spoke of, sorrowfully, as "the day they took the whalemen." The whalemen he referred to were a group of Quaker loyalists from Nantucket, who for some years operated a fleet of whalers out of Dartmouth, across the harbor from Halifax. They had twenty-seven ships cruising the South Atlantic, enough to keep two spermaceti factories going full time, as well as the cooperages and blacksmiths' shops needed to service the fleet. Then one day the British government issued a command invitation. The whalemen were to sail their ships across the ocean to Milford Haven and work out of that port in order to bolster Britain's whaling industry. So all but a few families moved to Wales, and their houses across the Narrows stood empty, their wharves idle.

Abraham Cunard had been shocked and saddened by Britain's high-handed expropriation of a thriving industry. He had joined the merchants in protesting against it. Britain had ignored the protest.

Sam was only five when the whalemen left, but all his life he remembered the August morning when their stubby little brigs had sailed in procession down the harbor and disappeared beyond the lighthouse.

Two years later, Halifax society was set agog by the arrival of tall, handsome Prince Edward, the Duke of Kent, who had been transferred from Gibraltar and made Commander-in-Chief of His Majesty's Forces in North America. This fourth son of mad old George III built himself an Italian villa on the shores of Bedford Basin, near the governor's summer residence. It was set in a three-hundred-acre park, with artificial pools and waterfalls, and many rare plants, and pasture for the duke's purebred horses. In this sylvan setting, Edward and his companion, Madame St. Laurent, entertained the dazzled citizens of Halifax with musical evenings and lavish suppers.

Sam's admiration for the duke amounted to hero worship. In the narrow streets crowded with soldiers, sailors, fishermen, West Indian traders, native Indians selling baskets, merchants on horseback, ladies in sedan chairs and rumbling drays loaded with cargo from the wharves, the duke's tall figure could be seen blocks away. Splendid in full-dress uniform, wearing a helmet topped with the lofty white plume of the fusiliers, he walked like a god.

It did not matter that instead of the royal playboy everyone had expected, Edward turned out to be a strait-laced martinet whose only vice was getting into debt, who put a stop to all-night card parties and had the officers as well as the men out drilling on the Grand Parade at the crack of dawn. He was a king's son, and his stay in Halifax was for years afterwards referred to nostalgically as "the duke's time," as if it were some golden age.

Life in the colonies had its grim side, too, in those days when the only highway was the ocean. The coastal waters of the world were still uncharted, and there were few lighthouses. Navigators went by hearsay, warnings about rocks and shoals being passed on from one sailor to another. Vessels crossing the Atlantic, headed for some safe port, often blundered into an unknown treacherous inlet a hundred miles away. The sailors who talked about far places also told stories of death and shipwreck. The Falmouth packets, running without lights, sometimes rammed into fishing schooners on the Grand Banks. Ships disappeared in mid ocean, were wrecked on the bleak rocks of Newfoundland, went down in the autumn gales that blew up from the Caribbean. Off the Nova Scotia coast, there were islands strewn with the timbers of lost ships and the skeletons of drowned men.

When Sam was ten years old the frigate *La Tribune* ran aground in a storm on Thrum Cap Shoals near the harbor entrance, so close to shore that the screams of the people on board could be heard from the mainland. All night, rescue boats tried to reach the sinking ship. The breakers stopped them all, and by morning 240 men, women and children had gone down with *La Tribune*. Eight were saved.

As the bodies washed up from *La Tribune* were carried ashore for burial, young Sam saw the horrors of shipwreck at first hand. The bodies had been dragged back and forth by the tide and battered against rocks. They were piled into drays and carted off to the burial ground for a mass funeral. The sight made a profound impression on him. The old sailors' tales took on new meaning as he realized, for the first time, how powerful an enemy the sea could be.

There were no public schools in Halifax, and only one private day school for boys: the Halifax Grammar School. The Cunard children were taught at home. In addition, Sam and the second boy, Will, were given a few years each at the Grammar School, where they were "instructed with the utmost assiduity and care in the English, French, Latin and Greek languages, writing, arithmetic, Algebra, Geometry, Astronomy, and Natural philosophy." Particular care was taken to "train up the pupils in a just pronunciation and graceful elocution." A dancing master led the boys through the movements and pauses of the minuet, to prepare them for future balls at the governor's new stone residence.

Sam was a bright pupil, good at figures; but he disliked the elocution classes and saw no use for Greek or Latin in either his own or Will's future. Some years later he explained to the headmaster of another private school to which he had sent his three youngest brothers, "the only reason I have for not requesting you to teach them Latin —namely, that they are intended for business, and a plain English education answers the purpose."

Sam decided very early that he was intended for business. When he had become rich and famous—"a sort of proprietor of the Atlantic Ocean between England and America," as one writer put it—old-timers in Halifax recalled how young Sam used to drive the cows home each morning and evening from Cunard's Field, knitting as he walked, fashioning a heelless sock with a drawstring at the top, similar to the moneybags carried by the merchants.

He had cash to put in the sock, having discovered that it was fairly easy for an industrious boy to earn money. People paid him to run errands and to carry letters to their friends. At the Merkel farm on the edge of town, where his mother sent him to buy vegetables, he was paid a few pennies to deliver produce to other customers. One Sunday afternoon when he was fourteen, he walked out to the farm to show "his first suit of broad cloth, earned by his own hand," to farmer Merkel and his wife.

Soon he learned how to make money work to earn more. In spring, he picked dandelion greens on the common after school. When he had sold them in the market, he took his earnings down to the wharves where the traders were auctioning off cargoes. Here he was able to pick up small bargains in coffee and spices, which he sold from door to door.

If he had been a poor boy, Sam would have made an ideal Horatio Alger hero. Like Ragged Dick and Tattered Tom, he was bound to rise. "It is a pity more lads do not follow his example," one journalist said of him later, "they might be a credit to their families."

Though they were far from rich, Abraham and Margaret were reasonably well-off by this time, able at least to employ servants—which could be had for a few shillings a week—to do all the work about the house. Certainly they would have been able to buy Sam's "first suit of broad cloth," if he had not been so anxious to prove that he could pay for it himself.

There was a reason for his overwhelming ambition to

make money, aside from the pleasure he got from buying and selling and trading—getting a foot in the door of the big, exciting world of commerce. All through his child-hood he had listened to stories of former grandeur, of the days when both his parents had lived in fine houses, big-ger and finer than any house in Halifax except the duke's villa. He knew these houses and their furnishings almost as well as if he had lived in them himself, though a few cherished pieces of pottery and china were the only tangible reminders of those better days. His father made sketches of delicate high-backed chairs and inlaid cabi-nets, intending some day to make duplicates of them. His mother spoke with such longing of the garden in South Carolina where her father had grown exotic fruits that most of her children, when they grew up, tried to recreate the dream garden of those old stories.

Sam wanted to give back to his parents everything they had lost. It was up to him, he thought, to restore the family fortune.

Sam was seventeen, and had left school and taken a job in his father's office by the time his youngest brother Henry was born in 1804. After a few years of drafting, copying, checking specifications for the masts and spars and timbers that went into ships of war, Sam left the lumberyard and boarded the packet for Boston, where his father had arranged for him to enter a ship broker's office.

This was no haphazard move from one job to another. Each step in Sam's education was carefully planned by his father. As he had prepared himself for exile twenty-five years before, Abraham now prepared his son for a career in shipping. Will, who wanted to be a shipmaster—a career that was highly regarded, since the captains usu-ally owned a share of the ship they commanded—went to sea at fifteen to serve his apprenticeship on a trader running to Martinique.

Will was the third young Cunard to go out into the world. In 1805—the year of Trafalgar, when the whole town celebrated Nelson's great victory—Mary, at twenty-one, had married an officer of the Royal Navy, Captain John Parr of the transport service, a native of Lancashire. Every girl in Halifax dreamed of finding a husband among the British officers stationed there, thus gaining entry into the more civilized world of English society. Commissions were bought in those days, and were only granted to young men of good family. Captain Parr was soon transferred back to England, where he was placed in command of a West India packet out of Falmouth. Mary, of course, went with him.

Sam spent three years in Boston, then only a small town, though it was growing in importance as a seaport. Since the Revolution, American shipping had increased so rapidly that Britain was in danger of losing her self-imposed title of Mistress of the Seas. Boston ships sailed to the Orient for tea and spices, and around the Horn to the new settlements in the Columbia River country where fur trading was carried on.

Sam was short and slight like his father, but strong and full of energy. He could dance half the night and be up at dawn the next morning looking as wide-awake as ever. In Boston, Sam made friends easily, went to parties and concerts and had a fine happy time, but he never lost sight of his goal, which was to learn everything there was to know about ships and shipping and world markets.

Letters from his father told of increasing prosperity in Halifax, as Britain's long series of campaigns against Napoleon continued. When the Peninsular War began in

1808, a few merchants prepared to reap even greater profits, running the French blockade with cargoes of food for the British troops in Spain.

Sam returned home before his twenty-first birthday. Abraham had retired from the lumberyard, built a landing wharf at the foot of Cunard's Hill and ordered a small schooner from Margaret's brother Tom Murphy, who had set up shipyards in Charlottetown, Prince Edward Island. Like their pioneer ancestors in Philadelphia, Abraham and his son started what was to prove a prosperous shipping business with one small coaster. The schooner *Margaret* carried trade goods between Halifax and nearby ports. The second ship, the *Nancy,* was a privateer's prize captured from the French off St. Pierre and put up for auction. With Will in command, she transported sugar and flour up to the settlements along the Miramichi River in New Brunswick, returning with dried fish for the West India traders.

The firm of A. Cunard & Son grew slowly at first. Abraham was a cautious man, lacking the energy and optimism to take chances. He had never been strong, and the long years of hard work had affected his health. In the spring of 1811, when a letter from Barbados brought the news of Mary's death at the age of twenty-seven, both he and Margaret grew old overnight.

As was usual in those days, Captain Parr's family often sailed with him on the long voyage from Falmouth to the West Indies on the mail packet. They were at Bridgetown, Barbados, in December of 1810 when an epidemic of yellow fever broke out. Within three weeks Captain Parr, Mary, their baby daughter Margaret, and eight members of the ship's crew were dead.

It was around this time, while his parents were mourning the loss of their daughter and her family, that Sam began to take over the management of business and family affairs, though he was careful to keep up the fiction that his father made all the decisions.

In 1812, when President Madison declared war on Britain, it was thought at first that trading between Halifax and the American ports would be suspended. This would have meant ruin for many small shipping firms, including Cunard's. Fortunately, New England wanted no part of the war. When the declaration was announced, all the ships in Boston harbor flew their flags at half mast. The New England states and the Atlantic provinces got together and devised a plan to protect their trade. Soon proclamations were issued giving safe conduct to certain "neutral" ships of both countries, so that essential commodities could be exchanged. Cunard's small fleet was one of the first to be granted a neutral permit.

So while British and American warships fought their battles all along the Atlantic seaboard, and privateers of both countries roamed the shipping lanes, raiding and capturing whatever came their way, Cunard schooners flying the neutral flag went about their business unmolested.

This was the lucky break Abraham and his son needed to speed them along the road to success.

One of the bloodiest sea battles of the war was the fight between the British *Shannon* and the United States *Chesapeake* off Boston Light. On a Sunday morning six days after the battle, the *Shannon* limped into Halifax with the captured *Chesapeake* in tow. When the ships had anchored, young Tom Haliburton scrambled aboard the *Chesapeake* with the rest of the Halifax boys. Years later, when he had become famous as the creator of Sam

The *Shannon* and the *Chesapeake* entering the harbor of Halifax on June 6, 1813.

Slick, the sharp Yankee peddler of *The Clockmaker* and *The Attaché*, Haliburton described the splintered timbers and the blood-soaked deck where gallant Captain Lawrence lay dead, covered with the Stars and Stripes. Lawrence's last words, "Don't give up the ship!" became the motto of the United States Navy.

Halifax was a boomtown during the War of 1812. Within one year, the population doubled, as more British troops moved in and more warships came in for refitting. Prices went up, and the merchants reaped fabulous profits.

Privateering was a lucrative business, encouraged by royal command as a patriotic duty. The most famous privateer out of Halifax was the *Liverpool Packet*, owned by Enos Collins, a former cabin boy who later became a business partner in a number of Cunard enterprises. The

*Liverpool Packet* captured fifty American merchantmen and brought them in to Halifax, where they were auctioned off under the supervision of the Admiralty.

So many captured vessels went up for auction that the market was glutted. In March, 1813, one sale included "twelve full-rigged ships, eight brigs, seven schooners, and ten or twelve other vessels, all with cargoes." A. Cunard & Son picked up one of the square-riggers at a bargain, and in July they advertised that the *White Oak*, "with good accommodation for passengers," was loading for London and would sail with the first convoy.

This venture into transatlantic shipping paid off so well that Cunard bought another vessel and sent it down to the West Indies with a cargo of dried fish to be traded for molasses and sugar.

The firm was prospering beyond Abraham's most optimistic dreams. He was content to stay quietly in the background, overseeing the accounts and the office staff, while Sam bought and sold cargoes and supervised the loading and unloading of ships. "Cunard's" had come to mean Sam Cunard to the merchants and traders they did business with. Along the waterfront Sam Cunard became known as a sharp businessman, who always got the best of any bargain.

Such an enterprising young man did not escape the notice of mothers who had marriageable daughters. But Sam had already picked the girl he wanted to marry. She was Susan Duffus, the pretty, dark-eyed daughter of William Duffus, who was one of the town's most influential merchants. In the summer of 1814, at the age of twenty-seven, Sam became engaged to Susan, and had more reason than ever to strive toward success.

He was up at dawn every morning, brimful of energy

and optimism, hurrying down to the waterfront with a
sockful of Spanish and American silver to buy fish and
timber for export. Paper money was unheard of. Though
prices were quoted in pounds and shillings, not much
British currency ever reached Halifax. The troops were
paid in Spanish dollars which Britain obtained through
trade with South America and the West Indies. Merchant
shippers like Sam Cunard, who traded with the United
States and Spanish American countries, as well as Britain,
had to deal with three kinds of currency—the pound ster-
ling, the American dollar, and the Spanish dollar. But a
clever trader, by keeping one step ahead of his competitors on the fluctuating values of the three currencies, could
often make a profit on the exchange. There were no banks.
Other merchants carried the heavy coins around in long
woven moneybags. Sam still preferred a homemade sock.
One of his clerks, armed with a club, walked beside him.
Only the most foolhardy merchant ventured along Water
Street alone with his moneybag. At night the money was
locked up in an iron strongbox.

By the end of the war, A. Cunard & Son had established
such a reputation for reliability, integrity and plain business know-how, that Cunard's Wharf was one of the bus-
iest along the waterfront.

# 2

Sam had known the Duffus family since childhood. Lieutenant James Duffus of the Royal Navy, Susan's half brother, had been one of his friends at the Grammar School. Their father, William Duffus, had come from Scotland as a young man to visit his friend Admiral Sir Charles Douglas, who was then in command of the fleet. Duffus had decided to stay and make his living in Halifax. He rented a warehouse and began to import shiploads of fine British cloth. Within ten years he had accumulated a fortune.

Later, he brought skilled tailors from England, opened a shop and hung out a sign, "William Duffus, Taylor and Habit-Maker." The shop, where military and naval uniforms were made to order, earned him another fortune during the wartime boom. The officers dressed like dandies, in skin-tight white breeches and short red tunics trimmed with gold braid. Duffus's shop could tailor a dress uniform to such perfection that the wearer could neither sit down nor raise his arm above a salute.

William Duffus was a tall, distinguished-looking man. His second wife Susannah was noted for her beauty. Mr. and Mrs. Duffus were accomplished riders and kept a stable of valuable horses. As a boy in the duke's time, Sam had often watched them riding on the common. Mrs. Duffus wore a full-skirted habit of scarlet cloth, and a white beaver hat with a feather.

They were still a handsome couple when their oldest daughter Susan married Sam Cunard one winter evening in the drawing room of the Duffus mansion, with the rector of St. Paul's officiating, and a host of relatives in attendance. The date was February 4, 1815, a month before official word reached Halifax that the war with the United States was over.

Old Robert Cunard, past eighty, made the rough winter voyage by schooner from Saint John to attend the wedding. He had been assured by letter that Susan would make an ideal wife for his clever grandson. She had a lively, affectionate disposition, was "refined in manners and mind," and had inherited much of her mother's beauty. She was twenty.

Only two of the Cunard boys, Edward and Joseph, attended Sam's wedding. Will was at sea and had taken fourteen-year-old John with him. The little boys, Thomas and Henry, were at a boarding school in Pictou, a hundred miles away. Their sister Susan, a bride of eight months, was on hand with her husband, Captain John Ray.

The Duffuses were clannish Scots people, famous for their hospitality. They made a grand occasion of welcoming their new son-in-law into the family. Duffus and other established merchants had followed Sam's spectacular business career with interest and talked about him in the coffee houses. He would go on to even greater success, they predicted. His judgment was sound, he was always ready when opportunity knocked. Mrs. Duffus, a strong-minded, capable woman, had more of a hand in arranging the match than Sam guessed. She admired him because he had many qualities that she herself possessed. His energy and optimism matched hers. She knew he would go on being a success because the idea of failure never occurred to him. He expected nothing but good fortune to come his way.

The wedding took place on a Saturday. At dawn on Monday morning, Sam was back at the waterfront as usual, directing the unloading of the schooner *Margaret,* just in from Jamaica.

He had built a plain four-story house on Brunswick Street, next door to his parents' home, where he could keep an eye on them and on his young brothers. The high east windows overlooked the Cunard warehouse, and the traders tied up at the long wooden wharf. Brunswick Street, once a country lane, had developed into a busy thoroughfare, lined on both sides with substantial town houses. In the yard behind Sam's house, the little settler's cottage where he was born had been turned into servants' quarters. The stables and coach houses were at Cunard's Field, a few blocks away.

Susan was not, fortunately, as clever and capable as her mother. Much as he admired Mrs. Duffus, Sam preferred to be the dominant one in his own home. Susan was warmhearted and gentle, devoutly religious like her grandfather Murdoch, who was a Presbyterian minister. She was delighted with her new home and with the furniture Sam had bought during his first visit to London the summer before his marriage.

One thing Susan had learned from her mother was the

art of hospitality. Her house soon became a family gathering place, a second home for her five brothers and sisters
and for the Cunard boys. Members of the Murphy family of Charlottetown—Sam's cousins—would sail around
to Halifax for a "winter visit" of six months or more, and
the Cunard cousins in Saint John would do the same.

Susan was devoted to her husband's parents. Both
Abraham and Margaret were failing in health. Margaret
had been past forty when her four youngest sons were
born. Now she was in her late fifties, and Sam had been
aware for some time that the activities and demands of
a young family exhausted her. Gradually, he had taken
over the education and upbringing of his brothers.

It had been his decision to send Thomas and Henry to
boarding school. The new academy at Pictou was said
to be a good one, but Sam was concerned that the little
boys might be unhappy so far from home. Henry was
only eleven. When John came home from his year at sea,
he was sent around to Pictou on the schooner to join his
brothers. He carried his first half year's board money in
his pocket, along with a letter from Sam to the headmaster.

"I shall feel much obliged if you will have the kindness
to supply the little wants of the boys from time to time,"
Sam wrote. "They will require as winter approaches
worsted socks, and strong shoes which can be had at
Pictou better than here, and any other things you may
conceive they stand in need of and that will add to their
comfort please order for them, and your draft on me at
sight for the amount shall be duly honoured."

Edward and Joseph had finished school and were being
trained for positions in the family business. Edward was
a quiet dependable boy of eighteen, much like his father.

Joe was quick and clever, with an outgoing personality that made him popular with everyone. All the Cunard boys were handsome, but Joe, who had inherited more of his mother's changeable temperament than the others, promised to be the best-looking and, next to Sam, the smartest. At sixteen, he was half a head taller than Sam.

The news of Wellington's victory at Waterloo reached Halifax in August, 1815, forty-six days after the battle. Napoleon had been defeated at last. For the first time in almost thirty years, England had no major war on her hands.

Soon after Waterloo, the naval force at Halifax was reduced to a few ships. The troops went home, leaving only the permanent garrison. The streets seemed deserted. None of the merchants welcomed the sudden quiet, Sam least of all, for peace meant the end of wartime prosperity at a time when he had hoped to expand the business to make room for Joe and Edward.

He looked around for new ways to make money. Before the year was out, he had made another voyage to London and had secured from the British Post Office Authority a contract to carry the mail to and from Bermuda once a month. This was the beginning of his long career in the postal service.

During the War of 1812, the Falmouth packets had delivered all the overseas mail for the British colonies to Bermuda, where the letterbags consigned to Halifax had been picked up by the first ship going in that direction. Often this was a Cunard trader on the way home from Jamaica or St. Kitts. When peace was declared, the packets returned to their prewar schedule, calling at Halifax and New York in summer, and delivering the mail to

Bermuda only during the four winter months. Bermuda complained so much about the change that the British government decided to inaugurate a mail service between Halifax and the islands.

Cunard's packet service, which began in the autumn of 1815, gave Bermuda the most reliable mail delivery in the colonies, though it was impossible to maintain any set schedule because the arrival of the English packet in Halifax was so uncertain. The packets were supposed to leave Falmouth on the first Thursday of each month, but did not sail until enough passengers had been signed on to make the voyage worthwhile. The crossing from Falmouth to Halifax, westward against the prevailing winds, took from four to eight weeks, and in bad weather sometimes even twelve weeks. The run back to England, with a following wind, was quicker.

The distribution of English mail from Halifax to the various outports of the colonies was even more uncertain. When the packet docked at Halifax, letters addressed to outports such as St. John's in Newfoundland were set aside to be handed, perhaps weeks later, to the captain of a trader bound for those ports. The sea voyage around the Gulf of St. Lawrence to Canada—which at that time consisted of the present provinces of Ontario and Quebec—was so long and difficult that it was easier to send the mail overland. The letterbags were carried by riders from Halifax to Annapolis, one hundred forty miles away on the Bay of Fundy, across to Saint John by ship, and up the Saint John River by canoe to where the overland trail began. Then the couriers went on foot, more than two hundred miles through swamps and forests, to a place on the St. Lawrence where the bags could be transferred to a ship going to Quebec.

Early in 1816, Cunard's contract with the British Post Office was amended to include mail delivery to Boston as well as Bermuda. After that, the Canadian mail was sent to Boston during the winter months. From there it was carried overland by dispatch riders, through Vermont and across frozen Lake Champlain to Montreal.

It took about a year for Halifax to feel the pinch of the great postwar depression—unemployment and hunger and beggars in the streets. There was hunger in Britain, too, and thousands emigrated to the new world, hoping to find a better life. They were packed into the dirty holds of the worst ships afloat, with rats and fleas for company, and those who landed in Halifax found that conditions were no better than at home—in fact they were worse, because the winters were colder.

But poverty was nothing new in the early days of the nineteenth century. All through the prosperous war years, one quarter of the population of Halifax had existed on handouts from the Poor Society. The poorhouse was crowded with old people and children. During the postwar slump, the well-to-do suffered no privations, and beyond contributing to the Poor Society not many concerned themselves with the sufferings of the jobless.

Susan, however, was acutely conscious of the misery outside her own comfortable home, and spent many hours collecting food and clothing for the immigrants. She was joined in this work by the governor's lady, the Countess of Dalhousie, who organized so many charities, and did so much to relieve distress, that she came to be known as "the queen of the beggars."

The countess persuaded the government to supply money for soup kitchens. She appointed Sam Cunard and an older merchant, Michael Tobin, as trustees of the

George Ramsay, Earl of Dalhousie.

fund. Each winter thereafter, for four years, Cunard and
Tobin set up soup kitchens near the Grand Parade, dis-
pensing hot broth and bread to about five hundred people twice a day.

As a result of Susan's work among the paupers, a life-
long friendship developed between the Dalhousies and
the young Cunards. George Ramsay, Earl of Dalhousie,
had been one of Wellington's generals. A keen agricul-
turist, he spent most of his term as governor of Nova
Scotia trying to promote more scientific methods of farm
management. He introduced cattle fairs and plowing
matches—which, to his dismay, usually turned into drinking matches—and handed out seed grain to poor farmers.
Under such distinguished patronage, farming suddenly
became fashionable. Many Halifax merchants bought
country estates, stocked them with cattle and horses imported from England and tried to coax vegetables from
the rocky soil.

The social life of the town went on as usual during the
depression, with entry into the charmed inner circle more
closely guarded than ever. The hostess who broke the
rules risked being ostracized herself. The bishop's wife
had more than once swept haughtily out of a ballroom
because she had spotted some new-rich upstart entering it.

As colonel of the volunteer Second Regiment, called the
Scarlet Runners because they wore such dashing red coats,
Sam presided over the social evenings which were the
militia company's chief activity now that the war was
over.

All the merchants belonged to one or another of the fire
companies, organizations dedicated to saving the town
when fire threatened to destroy it. The members of these
fraternities equipped themselves with leather caps and

William Edward Parry. As a young lieutenant, Rear-Admiral Sir William Edward Parry (1790–1855) spent four years at the Halifax naval base, arriving there on June 7, 1813, on the 74-gun *LaHague*.

canvas buckets bearing their club's insignia, and whenever a fire broke out—which was often, though smoking in the streets was strictly forbidden—they grabbed their caps and buckets and rushed off to put it out. There was great rivalry among the various clubs, each one trying to be first in the bucket brigade from the town pump. Sam belonged to the exclusive Sun Fire Company whose members were chosen by secret ballot. They met once a month to eat a seven-course dinner at the best hotel, and once a year they sponsored a great ball, a highlight of the social season.

A frequent visitor to the Cunard home during the postwar years was Lieutenant William Edward Parry—called Edward by his friends—who was stationed at the naval base. He was a friend of Susan's half brother, James Duffus, also a lieutenant in the Royal Navy. A long illness forced Parry to spend many months' sick leave in Halifax. His ambition was to discover a ship route across the top of the world from Greenland to the Bering Sea.

Sam had no way of knowing, as he listened to the young lieutenant's dream of finding a northwest passage, that his friendship with Parry would prove valuable twenty years later, when Parry had been appointed to the British Admiralty post of Comptroller of Steam Machinery and Packet Service. There was no such post in 1816. The phrase "steam navigation" was not often heard. Hardly anyone in Halifax had seen a steamboat, the odd vessel that was propelled by giant paddles going around like mill wheels on either side, though the newspapers reported that the invention was proving practical on inland waterways.

Parry, cruising the St. Lawrence on H.M.S. *Niger* in the summer of 1816, wrote that he had seen a steamboat, "a truly wonderful piece of mechanism," going down river at nine knots.

Steam navigation in America got off to a good start in 1807 with Robert Fulton's *Clermont,* running up the Hudson between New York and Albany. Two years later John Molson's eighty-five-foot *Accommodation* was put

John Molson's *Accommodation,* the first steamer on the St. Lawrence River. She made her first voyage from Montreal to Quebec in thirty-six hours, on November 3, 1809.

into service on the St. Lawrence, carrying passengers between Quebec and Montreal. She was later replaced by the larger *Swiftsure,* which was the "wonderful piece of mechanism" that Parry wrote about.

Britain's first passenger steamer had appeared in 1812— the *Comet* running between Glasgow and Greenock. Four years later the English newspapers reported that steamers were being used on short sea voyages: across the English Channel and from Glasgow to Belfast. In the United States, there was a regular service between New York and New London, Connecticut, and the first Great Lakes steamers had appeared.

In the coffee houses where they often gathered to talk business, Sam and the other merchants of Halifax discussed these developments. The steamer was a fine invention, they agreed, indispensable for anyone engaged in canal and river traffic. But they were deep-sea men. Their trade routes were on the ocean. None of them dreamed that steam vessels would ever threaten the supremacy of the ocean windjammers, the real ships, the big square-riggers on which world trade depended.

The new sailing packets of the Black Ball Line, which began running between New York and Liverpool in 1818, caused more of a stir in ocean shipping circles than any report about "steam kettles." The Black Ball people had come up with a new idea, a "line" of ships across the Atlantic. And their four packets ran on schedule, not just when enough passengers and cargo had been signed on. "Full or not full," one ship left New York and another left Liverpool on the first day of every month. They were the fastest ships on the Atlantic, averaging twenty-three days to Liverpool and forty days home to New York.

Even the famous voyage of the *Savannah* in 1819 did not impress the owners of ocean traders. The first reports said that the 110-foot steamer had crossed the Atlantic in twenty-five days from Savannah to Liverpool, where she was greeted as a nine days' wonder and her captain given a hero's reception. As soon as this news reached New York, a group of optimists there formed the Ocean Steam Ship Company, announcing immediate plans to build ocean steamers.

But when the excitement had died down a little, and the facts had been examined, it turned out that the ship-owners had been right to be skeptical. The *Savannah*— not even a real steamer, but a sailing ship equipped with collapsible paddle wheels—had used steam only at the beginning and end of the voyage; and she had taken longer to reach Liverpool than the sailing ships of the Black Ball Line. The Ocean Steam Ship Company quietly folded.

Sam's great ambition at this time was to build up a whaling fleet that would surpass those of New Bedford and Nantucket. The men of his father's generation still talked about the brief years of glory when the home fleet operated by the Quaker whalemen had kept pace with the ships of New England. Sam had never forgotten the day they sailed away for the last time, or the sadness he felt, probably because he had been told that a tragedy was taking place. Ever since then, whaling had been associated in his mind with romance and adventure. Since the war, he had begun to think whaling might be a profitable industry. The Nantucket fleet, reduced to twenty-three vessels in 1814, now numbered seventy ships and was still growing.

Outfitting a ship for a two-year cruise to the South Atlantic fishery was a costly business, and good whalemen were hard to find. Ordinary seamen would not do. They could not stand the monotony. After six months, the green hands were ready to jump ship at the first port. But a whaler could get to the northern fishing grounds and back in one season. In 1817, A. Cunard & Son outfitted the brig *Rachel* and sent her on a summer cruise to the Strait of Belle Isle. The voyage was a total failure. The *Rachel*, returning home with only ninety barrels of oil, ran into a storm off the coast of Newfoundland. She was driven ashore and broke up on the rocks, the crew barely escaping with their lives.

It was a disastrous beginning, but the next year Cunard's outfitted another brig, the *Prince of Waterloo*. This time they asked the government to subsidize the cost of a voyage to the southern whale fishery, pointing out that if the industry could be revived, the whole country would benefit. The request was granted, and the *Prince of Waterloo* was dispatched to the southern ocean. For a year and a half she patrolled the Atlantic from Patagonia to the Cape Verde islands, following the route of the old Quaker whalemen. She returned home with barely enough cargo to cover the cost of the voyage. The next year the *Prince of Waterloo* tried the northern whale fishery around Belle Isle, with no better luck than before.

Three failures in a row. Sam began to see why the New England whalemen had lately forsaken the Atlantic fishing grounds and were going around the Horn into the Pacific. Some took the long route, stopping for water at Tristan da Cunha, sailing on east past the Cape of Good Hope to Australia, then working their way through the uncharted islands of the South Pacific to the Sandwich group and home around the Horn.

These were long voyages of three years and more, requiring bigger ships. The cost of outfitting such a cruise was enormous. After three failures, Cunard's could not risk so much capital, especially since their request for another government grant was turned down.

But Sam did not abandon his dream of reviving the whaling industry in Nova Scotia. He only postponed it for a time while other matters claimed his attention.

By 1820, the worst of the postwar depression was over, in spite of the fact that Britain had made Bermuda the headquarters for the North American fleet and Halifax a subsidiary naval base. Business conditions improved slowly. Most of the merchants managed to scrape through the lean years, but William Duffus was bankrupt. He could have weathered the slump if his agent in London had not absconded with company funds. Duffus lost everything. He borrowed money to start again and was ruined a second time when his warehouse burned down.

Mrs. Duffus, determined to show that she could cope

with any situation, refused to accept help from her son-in-law. Instead, she turned the Duffus's big downtown home into a lodging house. But she tried to keep up appearances. The young officers who came calling on her daughters must never suspect that the upstairs rooms were let. So the lodgers came and went by the servants' entrance. The ruse fooled no one, and the traffic in and out of the side door made it seem as if something furtive was going on upstairs. Sam appealed to her children, and finally Mrs. Duffus was persuaded to give up her lodging house scheme and accept an allowance. Sam arranged a settlement of £300 a year, which was enough to live on in comfort and even some luxury in those days, when a clergyman making £200 (about $1,000) a year could afford to keep three servants.

So Sam took the Duffuses under his protection and welcomed the added responsibility. Though she had held out as long as she could, Mrs. Duffus gave up her place as the family wage-earner with apparent relief. Looking after roomers took up time which she would rather devote to Susan's babies.

The little Cunards were arriving at the rate of one a year. Edward was born on the last day of December, 1815, just as the town clock built in the duke's time was striking midnight. By 1821, four girls had been added to the family—Mary, Susie, Margaret, and Jane. In time there would be three more girls and another boy. A family of nine was not considered large in those days. Many parents brought up fourteen or fifteen children.

Mrs. Duffus, who had already brought up three families —her young brothers and sisters, her husband's children by his first wife, and her own five—was passionately devoted to her grandchildren. Sometimes when business took Sam to England for three or four months, the older children were allowed to stay with Grandmother Duffus. Her house was "the place above all others" where they loved to visit.

Abraham Cunard retired in 1820 to the Murphy farm at Rawdon, forty miles inland from Halifax, where it was hoped that the dry country air would improve Margaret's health. She had inherited this property from her father. In the thirty-seven years since Thomas Murphy took up his land grant, the backwoods settlement had developed into a prosperous farming community with rich meadows and grazing land. The farm was in a little valley, sheltered behind low hills.

But Abraham was not strong enough to superintend the field hands and stablemen at the Rawdon place, or to attend to all the details of planting and harvesting and keeping accounts. So Will gave up the sea and turned farm manager, with sixteen-year-old Henry as his assistant. Abraham devoted his retirement years to laying out flower gardens for Margaret. She was still homesick for her old home in the south.

Lord Dalhousie, on a tour of the district, stopped over for a few days to admire the horses and fat cattle. The sheep were descendants of a fine ram he had brought from his Midlothian estate in Scotland. Dalhousie, after a holiday in Scotland, was on his way up to Canada, where he would hold the post of governor for eight years.

Margaret lived to enjoy her country home for two summers. She died in late December, 1821. Abraham died two years later. He was buried beside her in the graveyard adjoining the little village church of St. Paul's in Rawdon.

# 3

After Abraham's death, the family business was reorganized. The name was changed to S. Cunard & Co., with Edward and Joseph as Sam's partners. Henry—back from the farm—and Thomas held junior positions. John, master of the brig *Mary Ann,* shared the profits of that trader, which carried fish and wood products to the West Indies, returning with puncheons of rum and hogsheads of sugar.

Other Cunard traders brought hides and coffee from South America. Big square-riggers carried timber to Britain, returning with cargoes of dry goods, food staples, sometimes even sheep and horses. Cargoes of flour, raisins, rum, molasses, coffee and sugar were shipped to Newfoundland and other outports. Passengers and cargo went to Boston and Bermuda on the mail packets. The Cunard brig *Chebucto,* under contract to the British government, patrolled the coastal waters to see that American fishermen stayed outside the three-mile limit.

The first flag of the Cunard fleet, a blue pennant with a white star in the center.

About thirty vessels carried the Cunard pennant. Each merchant fleet had its own signal flag, flown at the main-mast. Whenever a local ship was sighted off Sambro Light, the owner's flag was hoisted on the yardarm of the signal staff on Citadel Hill, which was visible from all parts of the town. Cunard's pennant was sea blue, with a big white star in the middle.

As long as his father was alive, Sam had been careful to seek his advice, and in other ways to pretend that Abraham was the real head of the firm. He had often wanted to embark on new enterprises, like the town's leading capitalist Enos Collins, who ran several businesses from an office in his warehouse on Water Street. Abraham had been timid about branching out, especially after the whaling losses, and Sam had not persisted. But for a long time he had been keeping an eye on the timber market in Britain. He had agents in London, Liverpool and Glasgow, and visited all three places periodically, always sailing on one of his own traders. In addition, he acted as colonial agent for several British mercantile houses.

Most of the fish and timber exported by Cunard's came from the Miramichi, a river in northern New Brunswick emptying into the Gulf of St. Lawrence. Twelve branch rivers flow into the wide Miramichi, draining thousands of square miles of forest. Lumbering had begun in that area during the war with Napoleon; Britain's usual wood supply in the Baltic had been cut off and she had turned to the forests of North America. Little towns had sprung up in clearings along the Miramichi. Behind and all around them, thick woods stretched for hundreds of miles, accessible only along the waterways of the branch rivers.

In 1812, the great Glasgow firm of Pollok, Gilmour & Co., the largest shipowners in the world at that time, had sent out two young men, Alexander Rankin and James Gilmour, to open a branch of their business at Douglastown on the north bank of the Miramichi. Gilmour and Rankin had built up a thriving export trade in timber and dried fish and had established shipyards. The ships they built were of tamarack, a buoyant softwood—nothing like the oak ships of England, but a good deal cheaper to build and popular with British buyers.

Sam acquired the timber rights to a large section of the King's Woods south of the Miramichi. He opened an office in Chatham, across the river from the Gilmour and Rankin works at Douglastown, and sent Joseph and Henry to run this branch of the business.

The brothers soon had gangs of lumberjacks and raftsmen in the river valleys. Cutting was done in the winter months. Teams of oxen hauled the logs over hard-packed snow to the rivers, where they were rafted down to the Miramichi on the spring floods. At the lumberyard, broadaxes were used to square the logs, which were then placed over a saw pit while two men, one above and one below, cut them into planks with a long two-handled lumber-man's saw. It took a long time to slice a log into planks, so Cunard's confined the bulk of their export to squared timber. The workers were not paid cash. They took their wages out in trade at the company store which Cunard's opened in Chatham.

Joe Cunard was a born go-getter. He tackled every-thing—taming the wilderness, bossing the gangs of tough lumberjacks, outsmarting his competitors—with a kind of dramatic intensity. By 1825 he had the Miramichi branch of the business well established.

All that summer, shiploads of timber went to Britain and the West Indies. In October, a great fire roared down from the north. The woods were tinder dry after a rainless summer. The flames advanced over a hundred-mile front, trapping thousands of wild animals, cooking the salmon in the rivers, burning the settlements in the clearings, and killing five hundred people, until it was stopped by the wide Miramichi.

Most of the ships anchored in the river escaped to the sea. A few were burned to the waterline. Gilmour and Rankin lost everything—all their buildings and stores of lumber, ships under construction in their yards, their fish-drying sheds. Even their homes were burned to the ground. The Cunard works at Chatham on the south side of the river were untouched.

Seven thousand square miles of timber had gone up in smoke. But there was still a seemingly limitless supply left. Within six months the lumbering industry was on its feet again. Within a year, Gilmour and Rankin were back in the race with Cunard's, stronger than ever.

The Miramichi branch of the firm had been in opera-

tion less than a year when Sam heard opportunity knock-
ing in another direction and made haste to investigate.

Britain's colonies were allowed no direct trade with
China. The East India Company's monopoly of India
trade had been abolished, but the famous old company
still controlled the China trade. London was the distributing point for China tea. Word had reached Halifax that
overseas agencies were to be established. Sam determined
to capture the North American distributorship. He had
already built a new warehouse, a dignified stone building
with oak doors, the firm name on plain brass plates such
as he had seen outside the offices of merchant bankers in
London.

Enos Collins, the former privateer now running a ship
broker's office and a private finance company in addition
to his trading activities, also had his eye on the tea
agency. Collins, who kept the current governor Sir James
Kemp in line by hinting periodically that he might remove
himself and his immense fortune to the United States,
thought he had enough pull to get what he called "this
Buiseaness which would be quiet and respectable, and
easily managed" simply by telling Sir James that he
wanted it.

Sir James did his best, but he and Collins were in Halifax, while Sam had gone to London where the action was.
Sam was so determined to get the agency that he could
not wait for one of his own traders. He sailed on the mail
packet *Cygnet* four days before Christmas, 1824. He
reached Falmouth in early February, and after a jolting
three-day journey to London by coach, arrived at the
Angel Inn behind St. Clement's Kirk in the Strand, where
all the west country mail coaches put up.

Because of previous business trips, he knew London

well by this time, and had no need to ask directions when he set off up Ludgate Hill toward Leadenhall Street, where the Honourable East India Company had its offices. He had walked that way many times before. It was in Paternoster Row, just off St. Paul's Churchyard, that he had bought the great family Bible, resting on a carved stand in the hall at home, in which he had recorded the birth dates of his children. The youngest, Ann, was now almost two years old, and another baby was expected in the spring. But one little girl, Susie, had died.

Landing the East India Company agency was not an easy job. Sam cooled his heels in London for five months before the contract was awarded to him. During this time he was not idle. He knew a number of people in the Colonial Office and through them he learned what policies were being considered for the Atlantic provinces. He was aware, six months before the report reached Halifax, that the King's Coal Mines in Nova Scotia had been turned over to the Duke of York and that a stock company in London had taken a lease on the mines. This knowledge enabled him to lay the foundation for still another branch of his business, though it would be several years before the mining company was well enough organized to use his services.

He visited the offices of merchant bankers in Lombard Street and learned as much as he could about their business methods. He bought books for the new public library in Halifax, which he had helped to establish in a room at the Provincial Building. Among the books he shipped home was *Journal of a Voyage to Discover a North-West Passage*, by William Edward Parry who, since leaving Halifax, had realized his ambition to lead an expedition in search of a sea route from Greenland to Bering Strait.

Lieutenant Parry had not succeeded in finding the Northwest Passage, but his ship had gotten halfway through before it was trapped for the winter in Arctic ice.

In June, with the East India Company contract in his pocket, Cunard sailed from Gravesend on his own brig *Susan*. When he reached Halifax thirty-six days later, his second son, William, was three months old. William was a more cheerful baby than his brother Ned had been, and since everybody said he resembled his grandfather Duffus, it seemed reasonable to expect that he would grow into a tall, handsome man.

Another year passed before the first East Indiaman sailed into Halifax with a shipment of tea direct from China. In the meantime Sam had invested in half a dozen other business enterprises.

He was invited to join a select group of moneylenders, including Enos Collins, to form the colony's first bank. The profits made by the shareholders of the Halifax Banking Company were enormous, but were condoned on the grounds that they "put a lot of money into circulation, which offered great convenience to those in trade."

"Before that," a Halifax resident later wrote, "drafts were not easily obtained, and travelers had to carry money. My father went to Montreal in 1824, and as it was winter he went by way of Boston, then by sleigh over the Vermont hills to Lake Champlain." His bag of American silver dollars, which he could never leave untended, caused him much concern on the long journey.

Though orders had come from England that the colonies must use British money exclusively, many people preferred the American dollar system. Some Spanish silver was still in circulation, too, as well as the metal tokens issued by individual merchants. Stagecoach fares, quoted in dollars and cents, were often paid in English shillings or Spanish pieces of eight.

The same group of merchant bankers formed the Annapolis Mining Company, where they lost some of the profits made in banking. They secured the mining rights to a small iron mine near the old French fort of Annapolis, and built a stone blast furnace for the manufacture of pig iron, which was made into stoves and kettles. Tom Haliburton, by this time practicing law and writing a book of history on the side, was dubious about the stove and kettle business. It remained to be seen, he said, "if they can compete with the English ware, or whether the cost of production will exceed the value of the article manufactured." The cost of production did prove too great, and the company failed, after spending £30,000, or about $140,000. As Haliburton's fictional hero Sam Slick remarked a few years later, "A man that has too many irons in the fire is apt to get some of them burnt."

A new epidemic of steamboat fever hit America in 1825, following reports that a British firm was about to start a regular steamship service between Ireland and New York—with a stopover at Halifax. Reports that the British *Enterprise* had steamed from London to Calcutta in 103 days added to the steamboat fever, though it was later learned that the *Enterprise* only carried enough coal for ten days. In Boston, a civic committee was formed to "promote the establishment of Steam Boat navigation between the port of Boston and the State of Maine and the British provinces." Plans included one steamer a week running between Boston and Halifax.

A few visionaries in Nova Scotia began to dream that Halifax might become the most important ocean terminal in the new world, the hub of Atlantic steam trade, with spokes radiating to England, Boston, New York and other ports. If this happened—and it seemed reasonable to suppose that it could, because Halifax was closer to Europe than any other American port—the town would grow and prosper as it had not done since Waterloo.

What was needed to complete the picture was a steamer service to Canada. Sailing vessels making the run to Quebec had such a hard time bucking the winds and currents of the Gulf of St. Lawrence, that there was not much commerce between the St. Lawrence ports and those on the Atlantic coast. A voyage from Halifax to Quebec took a month. A steamer might do it in a week. So the Quebec and Halifax Steam Navigation Company was formed; the three Cunard brothers—Sam, Joe and Edward—headed the list of shareholders.

Then, suddenly, there was no more talk about steamers crossing the Atlantic, and those who had scoffed at the idea said they had known from the beginning that it couldn't be done; that no ship, even if she carried nothing *but* coal, could carry enough to provide steam power all the way across the ocean. The Boston company shelved its plans for running steamers to Halifax.

The Quebec and Halifax Steam Navigation Company remained inactive for several years while the local newspapers tried to shame the shareholders into action. When the *Liberator* began to run between Boston and Portland in 1826, the *Novascotian* scolded: "It does seem a stain upon our enterprise that upon the harbors and estuaries of this province we have yet received no advantage from the most gigantic improvement of modern times—navigation by steam."

One of the earliest champions of the steamer was a young Halifax newspaperman, Joseph Howe, who later gained fame as a champion of the people's rights, a rebel against the established government. Howe wrote about the value of steam for towing vessels out of port. It was difficult for sailing ships to get out of Liverpool when the wind was blowing up the Mersey, but "an American packet which wishes to sail from Liverpool on a certain day, in place of waiting for a fair wind, employs a steam boat to tow her round the Rock—a service which is performed for £5, and hence the admirable regularity with which these vessels arrive and depart.

"There are upwards of 70 steamboats on the Clyde, and 50 on the Mersey," Howe reported. The latest coaster, the *United Kingdom*, launched at Greenock, was a "stupendous vessel," 175 feet long, with two 100-horsepower engines built by Napier of Glasgow, a spacious sleeping room for gentlemen, and a ladies' cabin containing "every convenience that luxury could invent."

But in Halifax, public interest had switched from steamboats to canals. It was an age of canal-building all over Europe and America. The Americans had just finished the Erie Canal from Albany to Buffalo, and in Canada the Welland Canal, to bypass Niagara Falls, had been started.

In Nova Scotia, where ships from Halifax carrying goods to the towns at the head of the Bay of Fundy had to beat around five hundred miles of rocky coast to reach a port that was only fifty miles away by land, people had been talking for years about cutting a canal across the province. Nature had provided a chain of narrow lakes strung north from Halifax to the headwaters of the Shubenacadie River, so all that was needed was a series of short canals connecting the existing waterways. But some lakes were up in the hills, and a survey had shown that it would take nineteen locks to get ships from one level to the other.

The Shubenacadie Canal Company was formed, with

Sam Cunard as vice-president. The sum of £85,000, or about $400,000, was raised. The work started out in a fine spirit of optimism. It was estimated that when the canal was finished, one small steamer would be able to tow four schooners up to the Bay of Fundy in less than a day. The voyage around the coast took almost a week.

The locks were to be built of native stone. Forty stone-masons, with their families, were imported from Scotland. The masons had built locks before and knew how to do it, but nobody told them that in Nova Scotia, where winters are more severe than in Scotland, frost penetrates deep into the ground. After each spring thaw the work they had done the previous summer heaved up and had to be repaired. Finally, at great expense, two locks were completed. Then a dam, built to hold back one of the upper lakes, burst and washed out all the work done so far. The company collapsed, having spent all its capital.

In the meantime, word had come from London that the East Indiaman *Countess of Harcourt* expected to leave Canton sometime in late January, 1826. If all went well, she should be rounding the Cape of Good Hope by late April. On May 29 the *Countess* was sighted off Sambro Light, and the signal flags went up on Citadel Hill. By the time she had picked her way past the ships lying at anchor in the harbor and reached her berth at Cunard's Wharf, all Halifax had gathered at the waterfront to greet her.

Captain Delafons and his crew of eighty had left Canton on January 25. They had touched at a few ports on the way—St. Helena was the last—for water and provisions. The *Countess* carried 6,715 chests of Bohea, Souchong, Hyson and other fine China teas, enough to supply all the North American colonies for a year. It took three weeks to transfer the cargo to Cunard's new warehouse.

Some of the tea was sold in wholesale lots, "at such prices as will effectually prohibit the contraband trade hitherto carried on to so pernicious an extent," the local paper reported, not missing a chance to rap the knuckles of those who had grown rich smuggling China tea in from the United States. "But we shall not be sorry," the report continued, "if the persons engaged in this traffic now find it to their interest to export tea from Halifax to the States." This was one way of saying that smuggling was only a crime when you were beating the revenue laws of your own country.

By July, the Cunard brig *Susan,* the schooner *Henrietta Cunard* and the mail packet *Lady Ogle* were carrying tea to Bermuda and the West Indies. Other traders supplied Canada and the colonial outports. Cunard's profitable agency lasted many years, even after the East India Company lost the monopoly of China trade in 1833. The annual arrival of the tea ship was an event of great importance in Halifax.

Cunard's profits from merchant banking, shipping, timbering, from the mail contract and the tea agency, were so great that his few failures were scarcely noticed. Now he was ready to try another whaling voyage. This time, however, he did not take on the whole cost of outfitting a ship himself. Twelve mercantile firms participated. The Halifax Whaling Company, a joint stock company headed by Sam, Edward and Joseph Cunard, was formed. The government had agreed to pay a bounty of £1,500 to "the first two vessels that may be fitted out in this province and employed for a time of not less than eighteen months in the Southern Whale Fishery."

The *Pacific* was launched in November, 1826. In two months she was ready for sea. She sailed from Cunard's Wharf in late January, bound for the South Pacific where the American whalers went. She was gone three and a half years.

Just before the *Pacific* sailed, Sam captured the prize appointment he had been trying to get for two years— he was named agent for the General Mining Association.

The King's Coal Mines, like the King's Woods, belonged to the crown. Anyone could engage in timbering or mining by obtaining a license from the government and paying royalties. There were vast coalfields in Nova Scotia, but mining on an extensive scale needed a good deal of capital, and though the demand for coal on the world market had risen with each new development in steam navigation, only one or two shallow pits had been opened up. They were worked by hand.

If the sons of old George III had not been so fond of getting into debt, the coalfields of Nova Scotia might have lain idle for another fifty years. Edward, that legendary figure of the duke's time, who died in 1820, left a mountain of debts which his daughter Victoria paid "out of her own private purse" when she became queen. In 1825 Edward's brother occupied the throne as George IV. Another brother, the Duke of York, had so many creditors hounding him that the king had to devise a way of appeasing them. He handed the King's Coal Mines in Nova Scotia over to the duke, who then passed the mining rights on to his creditors. They formed a company called G.M.A.—the General Mining Association.

The announcement that G.M.A. intended to work the coalfields, and had enough capital to set up the latest in steam equipment and machinery, was great news for Nova Scotia. Such an industry would boost the country's economy and provide work for a great many people. The coalfields were some distance from Halifax. One was on the East River near the port of Pictou on Northumberland Strait, another was in Cape Breton.

In January of 1827, Cunard's square-rigged ship *Margaret* sailed for England "in blustery weather from the north," and reached London sixty-one days later. She came home in June, loaded with the knocked-down components for hoisting and pumping engines—"the first steam engine ever affixed to our native soil," the local papers reported. The parts were taken around to Pictou and reassembled at the nearby Albion Mine.

As predicted, G.M.A. did employ a great many men, and they paid cash wages as high as $2.50 a day, when the going rate for a skilled shipwright was 90¢ worth of credit at the company store. G.M.A. accountants used the American dollar system because the best coal markets were in the United States. Sam Cunard, the sole distributor for this powerful firm, had his finger in a very rich pie.

He was already a wealthy man, with a fortune estimated at about one million dollars. The Cunard fleet numbered more than forty ships. The Duffus family fortunes had mended, too. With Sam's help, young John Duffus had reestablished his father's dry goods import business. Twice a year, John went to London and selected "a large assortment of goods suitable for the season"— enough to supply most of the retail merchants of the province.

Sam was constantly on the go, overseeing the various branches of his business empire. He sailed to Boston, New York, London, around to Pictou and up to Miramichi. He visited the outports. The short runs up and down the rocky coast in a small schooner, often against hard winds and rough seas, were his chief delight. He had great powers of endurance, could stand exposure to rain and wind and flying spray, and kept himself fit by dousing himself with cold water every morning, even on winter voyages, when the water pitcher in his cabin was half filled with ice. He had no time for the outdoor recreations other men enjoyed—hunting deer or fishing for salmon in the rivers or, in winter, taking part in the curling matches played on Smith's millpond.

At home, he assumed his share of civic duties, taking his turn as a committee member of the Poor Society, the Public Library, the Mechanics' Institute, acting as fire-warden and commissioner of lighthouses. On one occasion he had been persuaded to offer himself—"at the written request of the merchants and other respectable inhabit-ants"—as a candidate for election to the legislative as-sembly. He withdrew almost at once, however. He disliked public appearances and was a poor speechmaker; besides, he had an eye on the senior governing body of the province, the crown-appointed council.

Sam's days were all business and adventure and striving to get on in the world, while Susan's whole life revolved around her home and family. When her husband was at home, she presided at dinner parties and took part with him in the social life of the town; when he was away, often for months at a time, she had her children and a very large circle of friends and relatives to keep her occu-pied. She passed her own religious training on to her chil-dren. As in most Christian homes of the period, there were daily prayers and readings from the Bible, and church every Sunday, without fail.

The empty space left by the death of her second daughter, Susie, had been filled. When the wife of Sam's cousin Tom Murphy died, Susan had made a place in her home for Tom's little daughter Hannah, who was just three months younger than Susie would have been if she had lived.

Sam had begun to initiate his older son into his own way of life when Ned was not much more than ten. Ned often accompanied his father to Boston or to the outports. In December, 1827, the two sailed around to Pictou on the schooner to attend the opening ceremonies at the Albion Mine, when the marvelous new steam engine for hoisting coal was put into operation. Horse-drawn cars hauled the coal over a short rail line from the pithead to schooners docked at the riverside. Sam and Ned returned to Halifax on the stagecoach, in time for the usual round of crowded family parties. Christmas was always an occasion for sentimental get-togethers, arranged and presided over by Mrs. Duffus. Henry came down from Miramichi for two weeks. A romance had developed between him and Susan's youngest sister, Elizabeth, which was warmly encouraged by all the family. Ned was twelve that year. Susan—though her youngest child, Isabel, was less than a year old—expected another baby in January.

That was Susan's last Christmas. Her ninth baby, Elizabeth, was born on January 23, and Susan died ten days later.

# 4

All the Cunard and Duffus relations rallied round to help Sam bring up his motherless children. Susan's mother, who thought nothing of taking on a family of nine at fifty-six, naturally insisted that her son-in-law move his entire household into her home.

It took all Sam's diplomacy—what one of his friends described as his ability to "make both events and people bend to his will"—to dampen his mother-in-law's enthusiasm for this plan without losing her friendship. It was finally agreed that a better arrangement would be for the children to stay in their own home, with a competent woman to oversee the details of housekeeping, while Mrs. Duffus continued to act as a sort of adviser. This was essentially the way the household had been run all along. It had been Susan's mother, not Susan, who had trained the servants and engaged the nurses who looked after the younger children, and the governess who presided over the schoolroom at the top of the house.

"Dear Grandmother Duffus"—as the children always called her in later years, when they got together to talk about happy childhood times—was the beloved matriarch of the clan. Warmhearted, untiring in her management of family affairs, always first on the scene in sickness or trouble, she still rode every morning on the common, erect and graceful as a girl beside her tall husband.

The young Cunards grew up in an atmosphere of love and security, surrounded by an enormous number of aunts and uncles and cousins, each one determined to outdo the others in kindness. A sentimental group, they wrote to distant members of the family about the change that had come over Sam since his wife's death.

He had always been an affectionate and extremely generous father, never returning home without extravagant presents for everyone. Now, as if he regretted all the time he had spent away from them, he gave up traveling for many months, and devoted himself to his children. He became more conscientious in conforming to the religious behavior of the day, holding family prayers every morning at which the whole household was required to be present, all the servants included, as well as the coachmen and grooms who lived over the stables at Cunard's Field. With his children, he became a regular attendant at nearby St. George's Church. On winter mornings, maids went ahead with chafing dishes filled with hot coals to warm the family pew.

When Sam began making short voyages to the outports the following summer, he took the older girls as well as Ned with him. In the *Chebucto*, they made a tour of the lighthouses and stopped off at Pictou to watch the horse-cars delivering coal to the schooners.

Within two years, satisfied that the children were perfectly happy under their grandmother's supervision, Sam was on the move again. He was absent from home for weeks and months at a time. But he always took three or four children with him when he visited the outports. Sometimes the whole family would sail up to Miramichi to see Joe and Henry. Joe was still a bachelor, careless and fancy-free. Henry had married Elizabeth Duffus, and the two had bought a small country place on the river. They were quiet, home-loving people, fond of company. But they were not as exciting as Joe, who rode around like a king on a great black stallion, overseeing his work gangs.

On the way home, Sam and the children would stop off at Pictou to visit G.M.A.'s chief engineer, Richard Smith, who had been sent from England to run the Albion Mine. Smith had built an enormous manor house on a seventy-five-acre clearing in the forest, a little distance from the pithead of the mine. Mount Rundell, as Smith called the place, was like an English country estate set down in the middle of the wild backwoods, with massive gateposts, a gatekeeper's lodge and a grand sweeping drive running through parkland to a formal garden. Here Smith held open house for the important men of the province. Judge Thomas Haliburton always stayed at Mount Rundell when the circuit court was held at nearby Pictou. The judge was an old friend of the young Cunards. They often visited his home in Windsor, forty miles from Halifax, a rambling white house overrun with children.

That man of the people, Joseph Howe, also visited Mount Rundell. Years later Howe would play an important part in the abolition of G.M.A.'s monopoly of the coalfields. He had bought the leading Halifax newspaper, the *Novascotian*, and was beginning to attract attention with his editorials, the most famous being a series of articles lampooning the activities of His Majesty's Council, the senior governing body of the province, which Howe renamed The Club.

The British colonies were still governed the way the United States had been before the Revolution, with an elected assembly and a crown-appointed council. The council, composed of the twelve most influential citizens—supposedly selected by the governor, but in reality selected by one another—had power to veto laws passed by the assembly. Cunard supported this form of government. He believed, along with many of his contemporaries, that the man in the street had insufficient knowledge of the problems of government to select his own leaders.

When Cunard was appointed to the council in 1830, Howe and his friends were just beginning what was to prove a long battle to overthrow this governing clique. Members of The Club, Howe hinted, often took advantage of their positions to line their own pockets.

That year, the assembly and the council were involved in a controversy that became famous in local history as "the Brandy Dispute." The assembly discovered that the merchants who imported brandy into the province had for some time been taking advantage of a loophole in the revenue bill. They introduced a new, foolproof bill. The council, whose members included the bishop of Nova Scotia and import merchants Sam Cunard and Enos Collins, vetoed the new bill. But for once the assembly refused to accept defeat. The dispute went on and on. The existing revenue bill expired, customs authorities were unable to collect any duty at all, and the merchants benefited.

Joseph Howe lost no opportunity to satirize the situation. His newspaper accounts of the long impassioned debates in the House of Assembly, while members of The Club sat next door in the council chambers drinking duty-free brandy, hastened settlement of the dispute. The council members could not afford public ridicule. And the hints that they might be enjoying other hidden benefits caused them much embarrassment. After some months—and a great loss of revenue to the province—they decided to accept the new bill.

The defeat did not, however, make them aware of the growing strength of the reform movement. But the next year—when Cunard and two other council members went to London to protest the reduction of duty on timber from the Baltic, which affected the colonial timber market in Britain—they noted with alarm that a spirit of reform was abroad in England. "The nation itself," they wrote home, was in danger of collapsing over Lord Russell's Reform Bill, with "everybody lamenting the necessity of sacrificing the established institutions of the country and yielding to the popular voice, instead of rousing themselves to oppose it like Englishmen."

Cunard considered any departure from the old Tory traditions a step in the wrong direction. He was a charitable man, kind to the poor, considered "just but not generous" by his employees. But like Queen Victoria twenty years later—who found it "very touching" when an old lady to whom she had given a secondhand petticoat kissed her hand and asked God to bless her—Sam heard in the rising voice of the people only a threat against old-fashioned stability and ordered government.

Howe was all for encouraging the popular voice, though he was intensely loyal to the crown and had no wish to break away from Britain as the United States had done.

He was a born politician, an eloquent speaker and a gifted writer. He had never been, as he sometimes pretended, a barefoot boy. His father was the King's Printer for the Atlantic colonies and Bermuda. Howe could hold his own in the most brilliant company, but he could also talk to the backwoods people "like one of their own boys" about problems that concerned them. A stocky man with rugged features, he was outspoken, blunt, told pungent jokes and was always hard up.

How two men with such opposing views as Cunard and Howe ever became good friends was a mystery to all who knew them. Perhaps it was because of certain complementary qualities in each. Howe was a poet of some note, and Cunard was inclined, when in England, to mingle with London's literary set. A poor businessman himself, Howe undoubtedly admired Sam's ability to make money, though he never hesitated to denounce his methods, if he considered them too sharp.

The two men did share certain interests and ambitions. Both had visions of Halifax becoming a great world port and of Nova Scotia regaining her position as the most important colony in British North America, as she had been in the days before Waterloo. Cunard thought in terms of business, of the Cunard empire expanding and growing richer. Howe's concern was all for his country and its people. He wanted to replace the present government with a wholly elected government responsible for its own decisions, but with representation in the British parliament. His ultimate ambition was to represent his home colony in the British House of Commons.

Some of Howe's most caustic criticisms were aimed at the Halifax Whaling Company. The shareholders of this company, all men of considerable influence, had, in

Howe's opinion, pressured the government into offering a bounty on whale fishing at a time when they were the only ones in a position to take advantage of it. This was true, and Cunard and his friends did not deny it; but they were surprised that Howe did not recognize them as the community benefactors they believed themselves to be. Their motives were unselfish. They hoped only to build up an industry that would make the whole province richer—and if they grew a little richer themselves in the process, surely no one could deny that they were entitled to some return. In the meantime, the *Pacific*, the first ship of what they hoped would in time grow into a large whaling fleet, provided work for twenty-five local men.

The *Pacific* had been gone more than a year before Cunard received any news of her whereabouts. Then a letter came from the Bay of Paita in northern Peru. "We arrived at this place last Sunday after a voyage of nearly six months and a half," Captain George Pyke wrote. "We have only as yet got about 110 barrels of oil, which however they say is doing fairly well. There are one or two out from Nantucket these eleven months and have not got as much."

Later word, sent to Halifax by the master of an American whaler that had spoken the *Pacific* near the Sandwich Islands, was more encouraging. The *Pacific* had taken a thousand barrels of oil by that time. She came home with a full cargo. Her owners had already applied for and received the bounty.

In the meantime another whaler, the *Susan and Sarah*, had been dispatched to the South Seas. She was a Cunard ship, not jointly owned as the *Pacific* was. A year after she sailed, a smudged and water-stained note reached Cunard from "Aboard the *Susan and Sarah*, Pacific Ocean." It had been handed to the captain of a home-

bound New Bedford whaler, forwarded by him to Du-
blois & Co., Cunard's agent in Boston, and sent on to
Halifax on the mail brig. The *Susan and Sarah* had got
safely around the Horn, and was beating north toward
the coast of Peru, where her captain intended to hunt
black whales "until the season opened for sperm whale."
She had provisions for two more years, and would roam
through the unnamed Pacific islands as far as New Zealand, where the best sperm whales were found.

For twenty years, Cunard headed the Lighthouse Commission of Nova Scotia, where the British system of collecting maintenance dues from shipowners was used. The
*Chebucto*, leased by Cunard's to the government for
patrolling the fisheries, also made the rounds of the outports to collect the lighthouse fees.

When Cunard began his term of office there were only
half a dozen beacons along the shores of Nova Scotia. The
old Sambro Light off Halifax, built in 1759, was the first
one sighted by ships crossing from England. There was
no light then on Cape Race. Under Cunard's direction,
new lighthouses were built at the rate of about one a year.
He introduced the custom of painting each one a different
way—some plain, others with vertical or horizontal stripes
—to serve as day markers.

One of the most important beacons erected during his
term of office was the light on Seal Island, sixteen miles
off the southwest coast of Nova Scotia, where each year
dozens of little coasting schooners were lost with all
hands. Every spring, the mainland people went out to
Seal Island to bury the sailors who had died there and,
while they were at it, to salvage the wreckage and water-
soaked cargoes flung up on the rocky shores.

The little island, only a few square miles in area, often

obscured by fog, and in the path of changeable drift currents, was a menace to Cunard's own traders going to and from the New England ports and the Bay of Fundy. Just how great a danger Seal Island could be he was to learn a dozen years later.

The Seal Island beacon was lighted in late November, 1831. In the spring of that year, Howe's *Novascotian* had reported that "a great Leviathan of the Sea" had been launched at Quebec. This was the 160-foot steamer *Royal William*, owned by the Quebec and Halifax Steam Navigation Company, formed in 1825 and headed by the three Cunard brothers. The shareholders had finally decided to inaugurate a steam service between Halifax and Quebec.

For the past five years, Howe had been writing editorials urging the shareholders of this company, as well as the individual shipowners of Halifax, to start building steamers. He pointed out that in England, in America, and even up in Canada, the steamboat was in general use on the rivers and coastal waters, while in the whole of Nova Scotia there was only one vessel run by steam—a three-horsepower ferry that wheezed back and forth between Halifax and Dartmouth. With the launching of the *Royal William* and the promise of a regular steamer service between Halifax and Quebec, Howe was confident that Halifax would begin to regain its lost prestige as an important colonial seaport.

The *Royal William* made her first run from Quebec to Halifax in six days. This included a stop at Miramichi. Sam, with fifteen-year-old Ned, arrived from Boston on the *Emily* in time to join the celebration when the steamer docked at Cunard's Wharf on August 31, 1831. Sam spent hours aboard the steamer, asking questions and taking

The *Royal William*, after an oil painting by S. Skillett in 1834.

notes. She was a side-wheeler with two engines of eighty horsepower each and with one tall stovepipe funnel. Like all the early steamers except the Mississippi River boats, she was bark-rigged and could switch to sail if the engines gave out.

Earlier that year, in England, Cunard had taken his first train ride on the new steam railroad between Liverpool and Manchester. The *Royal William* convinced him, he said, that "steamers, properly built and manned, might start and arrive at their destinations with the punctuality of railway trains on land."

He immediately ordered two steamers for his own fleet. He had obtained a contract to run a weekly mail service between Pictou and Charlottetown in Prince Edward Island. The *Pocahontas* was built in England for this service and began running in 1832. The next year Cunard leased the *Pocahontas* to G.M.A. and put a larger steamer, the *Cape Breton,* on the mail run. The *Cape Breton* was also built in England. She made the voyage from Plymouth to Halifax by sail in forty-four days.

The *Royal William* continued to run between Quebec and Halifax until December, 1831, when ice closed the St. Lawrence port. The next spring a cholera epidemic in Quebec delayed all sailings until June. The steamer left for Halifax on June 16, 1832. When she reached Miramichi three days later she was flying the yellow flag, the signal that there was cholera aboard. Six crew members were down with the disease, and the captain was dead. The ship was put in quarantine. After a month she went on to Halifax, where she was again quarantined. She returned home in mid-August and lay idle for the next six months.

The year's lost revenue had bankrupted the company. In the spring, the steamer was sold to pay off the creditors. A few of the original owners banded together and bought her. But they had given up the idea of establishing steamer service between Halifax and Quebec. Their plan now was to sell the *Royal William* in England.

It is doubtful whether any of them knew, when they decided to send her all the way to London by steam, that the little Dutch steamer *Curacao* had already crossed the ocean twice, from Antwerp to the Dutch West Indies, for this fact was little known outside Holland. They believed that the *Royal William* was the first ship ever to attempt an Atlantic crossing by steam alone. She was sent around to Pictou to take on coal.

She sailed from Pictou on August 18, 1833, with thirty-six crew members and seven passengers. Her cargo consisted of "one box of stuffed birds, six spars, one box, one trunk, household furniture, and a harp." She carried 330 tons of coal.

Two months later a report arrived from her captain, John McDougall, saying she had made the crossing without serious mishap, though having run into a "gale of wind" on the Grand Banks she had lost her foremast and the use of one engine, and the engineer had reported she was sinking. "Things looked rather awkward," Captain McDougall wrote, "however we managed to get the vessel cleared of water, and ran by one engine after the gale ten days. After that we got on fairly well, and put into Cowes to clean the boilers." The next day, they went on to London, where the vessel was sold to the Portuguese government.

The voyage from Pictou to the Isle of Wight had taken seventeen days. An American sailing packet out of Boston had crossed to Liverpool in slightly better time, running before a gale all the way; but the performance of the *Royal William* convinced certain shipowners in Britain that crossing the Atlantic by steam instead of sail was not only possible but practical. A steamer could be expected to make the same time on every voyage, not just when the wind was right.

The stage was being set for the great revolution in ocean navigation. But the curtain would not go up for another five years.

During that time the Cunard enterprises in the colonies went through a period of change and adjustment as some branches of the business declined and others prospered.

The Boston and Bermuda mail contracts had grown more profitable since the schedule had been revised, with the overseas packets delivering the mail to Halifax all year round. Trade with the West Indies had fallen off. After the abolition of slavery in the islands, the cost of running the great sugar plantations had risen so high that trading fish and timber for those commodities no longer paid off. Imports of China tea had risen to spectacular heights, then declined. By the time the East India Company's monopoly of China trade was abolished in 1833, the imports had dropped to around three thousand chests a year. Cunard continued to act as agent for the East India Company, but now anyone could bring in tea from China. The big money days were over.

As distributor for G.M.A. coal, Cunard's profits were growing each year. Production at the Albion Mine had risen so high that a railroad for steam locomotives was started, from the pithead to the docks at Pictou six miles away. This line, the first steam railroad in the Atlantic provinces, would take four years to build. Hills would have to be leveled down, valleys filled in, and bridges built. The earth-moving equipment consisted of teams of oxen and men with shovels.

S. Cunard & Co. had started a retail coal business in Halifax, offering "speedy delivery from forty wagons with a minimum of delay." New stables were built at Cunard's Field, and about seventy-five draft horses kept there.

G.M.A. had opened up the mine at Sydney in Cape Breton and built a three-mile rail line to the waterfront, where horse-drawn cars delivered five hundred tons of coal a day to the waiting ships—"from the wagons directly into the hatchways of the vessels," the official announcement boasted. The whole Cunard family went up to Sydney on the steamer *Cape Breton* for the opening of the rail line in 1836.

Joe Cunard had bought up his brother's interest in the Miramichi firm and changed the name to Joseph Cunard & Co. Henry stayed on as his manager. Joe had outstripped his business rivals, Gilmour and Rankin. He owned a packing plant for fish, brickworks, stores. He built the first steam sawmill in the province and a gristmill. In 1833 Joe married Mary Peters, the daughter of a local government official. Relatives from far and near converged on Miramichi for the wedding, a spectacular affair that was the talk of the town for months afterwards.

Everything Joe did was spectacular. Following the example of G.M.A.'s Richard Smith, he built a magnificent home in Chatham, surrounded by formal gardens with statuary and strutting peacocks. On Sundays he was the lord of the manor, driving out with his wife in an elegant coach and four, a coachman up front and a footman behind, both in scarlet livery—a strange sight in that raw frontier town where the stumps of trees felled by the first settlers had not all been cleared away. On weekdays Joe was the hard-riding boss of the timber gangs. Flanked by six outriders, he galloped back and forth supervising the work gangs along the riverbank where boom crews and straining teams of oxen were towing the timber rafts to the sawmill.

Joe went to England once a year to see his agents in Liverpool. Each time he returned, with enough orders for fish and timber to keep the town working for another year, he was welcomed home with church bells and cannon salutes. The whole town of Chatham was employed in one or another of his enterprises, but that was not enough to make him a hero. His reckless go-ahead extravagance and flamboyant personality lent a kind of folklore magic to the harsh pioneer life.

Sam had always been considered the smartest of the Cunard boys, the leader who pulled the others along in his wake. Now people began to think that Joe might out-

strip his conservative older brother. He looked more successful. Sam still lived in the big solid house on Brunswick
Street overlooking the warehouses at Cunard's Wharf.
Though it was richly appointed inside, with books and
furniture and fine china brought back from England, the
house was not half as imposing as Joe's.

Business now took Sam to England every winter, too.
It had become routine for the older girls to accompany
him, two at a time. Joe usually sailed with the party,
which left Halifax soon after Christmas. Joe returned home
in April, Sam and the girls in June. The brothers were still
partners in a number of subsidiary concerns, including a
"land settlement" company which was not yet active.
Large tracts of land, mostly grants from the crown, were
being held for future development.

Sam visited his agents in Glasgow and Liverpool, but
spent most of his time in London, where he kept a suite
of rooms at a Piccadilly hotel and had a small office in the
G.M.A. headquarters on Ludgate Hill. The girls were
placed in a convenient private school, where they took
lessons in French, German and deportment. A "plain
English education" did not answer the purpose for Sam's
children.

Joe always spent some weeks in London seeing his
bankers—he ran his business on borrowed money—and
sharing his brother's social life. Sam knew many people
of rank: directors of the General Mining Association and
the East India Company, former governors of Nova
Scotia, senior officers of the army and navy who had been
stationed at Halifax. James Ramsay, the son of his old
friend Lord Dalhousie, was living in London with his
wife, who was a daughter of the marquis of Tweedsdale.

Joe had no opportunity, in the wilds of Miramichi, to

mingle with such distinguished people. In London he managed to meet most of his brother's friends, and impressed them all with his lordly charm.

Sam belonged to the old-fashioned, formal, compliment-paying school of courtesy. He had a large circle of women friends, including the tragic beauty of London society Caroline Norton, one of the three talented granddaughters of the dramatist Richard Sheridan and a writer of note herself. Her friends included such members of the literary set as the Irish poet Thomas Moore and Benjamin Disraeli, then better known as a novelist than a statesman. Mrs. Norton's husband scandalized England by publicly accusing his wife of carrying on with Lord Melbourne, the prime minister.

The scandal, which made headlines in 1836, was reported in minute detail in the Halifax papers, with hints that "the *faux pas* lady"—Joseph Howe's description of Mrs. Norton—was a particular friend of a certain local person. "Truly this is a wicked world," Howe wrote. "A dozen times we have turned over the pages of *Undying One and Other Poems,* by the Hon. Mrs. Norton in the Halifax library, but somehow or other we always resisted. The moment, however, that a rumor arose that the poetess and her husband were about to part—that a trial was talked of and the damages laid at £10,000—and that the consequence of a conviction might be the exclusion of Lord Melbourne from Court and the dissolution of his ministry—then the little volume possessed a singular attraction."

Norton's accusation—actually a smear campaign instigated by Lord Melbourne's political enemies—was quickly judged false, and Mrs. Norton's character remained untarnished. But in his hometown Sam found that he had acquired a reputation, by association, as a man of rather worldly experience.

His relations in Halifax were naturally alert for any indication that he was considering a second marriage, but Sam never met anyone who could take Susan's place. He was too busy to spend much time looking.

In September, 1837, the family gathered for the wedding of Sam's oldest daughter, Mary, to James Peters, a New Brunswick barrister. Four hours after the wedding, when the tide turned, Sam was off on the *Cordelia* to attend some pressing business in Boston, leaving his mother-in-law to speed the departing guests.

Having devoted herself to the care and upbringing of her Cunard grandchildren ever since their mother's death, Mrs. Duffus suddenly found herself, in 1836, with a new young family on her hands. She was sixty-four and her husband was past seventy when their second daughter, Mary Anne Morrow, died, leaving, as Susan had, a family of nine children. This time Mrs. Duffus persuaded the bereaved father to give up his home and move into hers.

Grandmother Duffus had taken the new family under her warm capable wing with her usual lack of fuss and scarcely a pause in her other activities. Fortunately there was plenty of money. She could hire as much help as she needed to run two households. Mary Anne's children were young enough to be turned over, for the greater part of each day, to nursemaids and governesses. The older Cunard girls, on the other hand, were at an age when their whole future depended on wise supervision and guidance.

Hannah Murphy, the cousin who had made her home with the Cunards for so many years, had gone up to Miramichi to live with Henry and his wife. Mrs. Duffus was keeping an eye on the young men of the town as possible husbands for Margaret and Jane, aged seventeen and sixteen, who were lively, pretty girls with brown eyes and dark curls. She gave a series of parties and invited all the best-looking young officers of the garrison and the fleet, being careful to exclude any who were known to be penniless younger sons.

That winter it was Willie's turn to accompany his father to London. As the only boy in a houseful of girls—for Ned was past twenty-one now, rather stuffy and superior, in his brother's opinion, and vain about his looks—Willie occupied a privileged position in the family. His grandparents doted on him, his father and the girls spoiled him. He could wrap anyone around his little finger, even Ned, who shot him looks of disapproval when he made his sisters laugh during morning prayers.

Sam Cunard was fifty years old when he sailed from Halifax in early January, 1838, with his brother Joe and his son William, who was not quite thirteen. Sam's hair was gray, beginning to recede from his broad forehead. Though he had grown a trifle portly, he still had more energy than many men half his age, and he walked with a brisk step, giving an impression of scrubbed fitness.

A middle-aged man with a benevolent expression, always immaculately dressed in a cutaway and a high white cravat, he had reached the goal he had set for himself when he was fourteen. He had made a comfortable fortune, and all his friends thought he had lost his youthful enthusiasm for risking capital in new enterprises. They were wrong. He was simply waiting for opportunity to knock again.

# 5

In England, three shipping companies had decided to try the daring experiment of sending steamers across the Atlantic to America. Three "mammoth" wooden side-wheelers were under construction: the *Great Western* in Bristol, the *Liverpool* on the Mersey and the *British Queen* on the Thames. These were the first steamships ever designed for ocean travel.

Building went on at top speed. Each company was determined to be the first to send a steamer to America, while some of the best engineers and scientists of the day warned that such a thing was impossible.

The most ominous predictions of disaster came from a scientific writer and lecturer, Dr. Dionysius Lardner, editor of *Lardner's Cabinet Cyclopedia* in 134 volumes. In fair weather, it might be possible for a steamer to cross the Atlantic from west to east with the prevailing winds, Dr. Lardner conceded; but to cross the other way, against the eastward-running Gulf Stream, the "violent atmospheric convulsions" of the trade winds, and the waves "hurled with accelerated momentum over a tumultuous confluence of water three thousand miles in compass," was an utter impossibility.

He pictured the firemen—who, he said, could never stop shoveling coal into the furnaces for one minute—dying of exhaustion in mid ocean as they tried in vain to keep up enough steam to combat these forces of nature. As a clincher, Dr. Lardner prepared an imposing set of figures which proved conclusively that not one of the steamers under construction could carry enough coal to run its engines the three thousand miles to New York.

In spite of these warnings, the steamship companies went on building. When Cunard reached England in early February, 1838, both the *Great Western* and the *Liverpool* had been launched. At the Thames shipyard where the *British Queen* was under construction, he found her still on the stocks—a 275-foot giant, so big, and with such a deep keel, that he wondered how she would ever be got off the ways. Later, he went up to Liverpool to inspect the much smaller *Liverpool* and stopped over at Bristol for a look at the elegant luxury steamer *Great Western*. She had been launched the previous July and was almost ready for sea.

By March, the *Great Western* was finished. It would be another year at least before the *British Queen* was ready. But her owners had no intention of giving up the race. They chartered the 178-foot *Sirius*, which had been built to run between London and Cork.

"The *Sirius* is actually getting under way for America," the London *Times* reported when she sailed from Cork on April 4. The *Great Western* left Bristol four days later. The *Times* obviously did not expect either vessel to succeed in "this long talked of project of navigating the Atlantic Ocean by steam."

But the vessels did reach New York. Early on the morning of April 23, 1838, the *Sirius* anchored in the Hudson off the Battery. Her arrival caused a sensation. Thousands of New Yorkers rushed down to the Battery. Every small boat on the waterfront was employed to carry sightseers out for a closer look at the spectacular ocean steamer.

The arrival of the *Great Western*, later that same day, was an anticlimax. She had made better time than her rival, but the *Sirius* had copped the prize as the first steamer from England to America. "Nothing is talked of in New York but about this *Sirius*," the next day's papers reported, "and a glorious boat she is. Every merchant in New York went aboard her yesterday."

Three mornings later, the Royal Mail packet *Tyrian* reached Halifax from New York, with news of the safe arrival of the two Atlantic steamers.

The *Tyrian* sailed for Falmouth on the night tide, carrying more passengers than usual. Most of them were bound for London and Queen Victoria's coronation in late June. Joseph Howe and his friend Judge Haliburton were aboard. Howe had been elected to the legislative assembly, a better position from which to carry on his campaign for "responsible" government. Judge Haliburton, a tall handsome urbane gentleman of smooth wit, a loyal Tory, held the dignified position of chief justice of the common pleas in Nova Scotia. But in 1835 Haliburton had written a series of satirical sketches for Howe's *Nova-scotian* about a "genuine Yankee" peddler of clocks ($40, marked up from $6.50) named Sam Slick. This parody of American manners and customs was later published in London and Philadelphia under the title *The Clockmaker, or The Sayings and Doings of Sam Slick of Slicksville.*

The book was an instant success in both countries. A second Sam Slick book was to be published in London that summer.

This was Howe's first trip abroad. Before he returned home he would number Dickens, Thackeray and other literary greats among his friends. Aboard the *Tyrian,* "in a small stateroom six by four," he wrote the first of a series of articles about his journey to the Old World.

"Under the influence of light and variable winds we have passed the Isle of Sable, skirted the Gulf Stream, caught a Halibut on the Porpoise Bank, and some fine cod on the Banks of Newfoundland, and have been driven on for several days by half a gale from the north, until here we are, just midway between the Old World and the New." They had been out two and a half weeks and had sighted one ship, a French schooner from St. Pierre fishing on the Banks.

A few days later the wind died. The *Tyrian* was drifting along with idly flapping sails when a smudge of smoke was sighted astern. Every passenger rushed to the quarterdeck to see that marvel of modern engineering, a steamer in mid ocean. "On she came in gallant style, with the speed of a hunter, while we were moving with the rapidity of an ox-cart loaded with marsh mud. Is it the *Sirius?* Can it be the *Great Western?* At last she ranged up alongside." It was the *Sirius,* two weeks out of New York.

The steamer expected to reach Falmouth within two days, then she would go on to London. The *Tyrian* might be stuck where she was for another week. The packet captain decided to send the mailbags ahead on the *Sirius.*

Howe "got a seat on the mailbags and while they were being handed up had five minutes of chat with the passengers on the quarterdeck and took a glass of champagne

with her captain in the cabin." One of the passengers was
James Gordon Bennett, who had come to Halifax as a
poor immigrant from Scotland and had taught school
there until he saved up enough money to move on to New
York and start a newspaper—the New York *Herald*.

"Now that the experiment has been fairly tried," Howe
wrote, "there can be little doubt that ere long the Atlantic
will be aswarm with these sea monsters, and that a complete revolution will be wrought in the navigation of the
ocean, as has already been witnessed on the rivers and
inland seas."

He considered the benefits to Halifax if the Atlantic
steamers could be induced to stop at that port on their
way to New York. "Immigrants would come out," he
wrote. "And if the Government was disposed to patronize
the undertaking, the public mails and dispatches could
also be forwarded, in charge of an officer, at much less
expense than the present dilatory and costly system."

He talked this over with Haliburton and other passengers from the Atlantic provinces. They estimated that the
British government could send the overseas mail to Halifax on one of the steamers—either the *Great Western*
or "that still more monstrous creation" the *British Queen*,
when she was finished—for about half the cost of operating the sailing packets.

They decided to do some scouting to see how the
steamship companies felt about stopping at Halifax once
a month. From Falmouth, Howe and Haliburton went up
to Bristol and talked with the owners of the *Great Western*, while another Halifax man went to see the owners of
the *British Queen*.

England was still buzzing with excitement over the
Atlantic steamers. The first news of their arrival in New
York had been brought back by the *Sirius* herself.

In London, Cunard and his son were awaiting word that their ship, loading at Gravesend, was ready to sail for home. Willie had spent four months under the care of a French professor who boarded half a dozen boys at his home on the Knightsbridge High Street, near the Rose and Crown. Willie had not been particularly happy there. But his last week in London, when his father took him around to see the sights, made up for everything. They went to Hampton Court by omnibus to see the maze and spent a day at Kew Gardens. Willie had never dreamed that such gardens existed. Years later he would try to create, in other places, some of the enchantment of those landscapes.

When Howe arrived in London on May 29, he went immediately to Cunard's hotel at 206 Piccadilly. Over dinner that night, the two had a long discussion about the ocean steamers. The Great Western people, Howe said, had "expressed their willingness to put boats on the direct line to Halifax, provided the British government would give them the carriage of the mails." The owners of the *British Queen* had said they would consider a similar proposal. One of Howe's friends, a member of the New Brunswick legislature, had written a letter to the Lords of the Treasury, urging that the Falmouth packets be scrapped and the mail sent to Halifax by steamer.

After dinner, Howe went off to see *Othello* at the Drury Lane Theatre (with its "vast splendid chandelier,") while Sam entertained more of his friends from home. They talked of nothing but the wonderful new ocean steamers —of the *Great Western*'s amazing record of fifteen days from Bristol to New York, and how the fast delivery of English market reports would benefit the New York merchants.

Cunard and his son William left London the next evening. They carried the usual number of "home letters," as well as Howe's dispatches for the *Novascotian*. The voyage to Halifax took more than a month, a time of enforced idleness, with no news of the world. Cunard had plenty of time to think.

The British postal system was undergoing a major revision that year, following publication of Sir Rowland Hill's *Post Office Reforms*. Hill had recommended a uniform postal rate of one penny for letters delivered within the United Kingdom and the use of the "postage stamp," a small bit of paper glued to the back of a letter to show that the cost of delivery had been paid.

But the biggest change so far was in the ocean post. Before 1833, all the mail packets running between England and the continent had been owned by the crown, not, as in the North American colonies, by private shipowners under contract. A change was made that year, however. Contracts were let to a few private steamship companies, which were paid an annual "subsidy" for carrying the mails to Ireland and the continent. They gave such good service that it was decided, over a period of time, to replace all the crown-owned coastal packets with steamers operated by private owners.

Britain was looking for a way to keep up her naval strength without going to the expense of building warships, so all the contracts with private owners specified that if war broke out the mail steamers were to be leased to the Admiralty and used as troop carriers. At the beginning of 1837, the whole packet service had been turned over to the Admiralty, and Sir Edward Parry was made Comptroller of Steam Machinery and Packet Service. His job was to hasten the conversion of the packet lines to steam.

But Parry would not consider scrapping the old Atlantic sailing packets until he was quite certain that crossing the ocean by steamer was safe and practical, Cunard thought. The *Sirius* and the *Great Western* had made one return voyage each, in fair weather, which did not prove that they could do it ten times, through heavy seas. If either of these ships met with an accident in mid ocean, the public would be quick to condemn the new method of Atlantic transportation.

The public was already up in arms about the high accident rate on the coastal steamers. Exploding boilers, fire and collision, in that order, headed the list of causes. Harrowing newspaper accounts of these disasters—the "excruciating agony of the victims" when the boilers exploded and scalded them to death, the "utter confusion and terror" when fire broke out aboard ship, the crash "more terrific than words can express" when two fast-running steamers collided—did nothing to build up public confidence.

But Cunard was convinced that once people had learned to trust the ocean steamers, the Atlantic would be, as Howe put it, "aswarm" with them. He agreed with Howe and the others that it would be a good thing to have the overseas mail delivered to Halifax by steamer, but he thought they were wasting their time writing letters, as they had done, to the lords of the treasury, and as they contemplated doing, to the colonial secretary, about a matter that should be taken up with the Admiralty—specifically, with the new Comptroller of Steam Machinery and Packet Service, Sir Edward Parry. Cunard had not seen Parry for twenty years, but remembered him as a pleasant earnest young man. Now, of course, he would be approaching fifty.

Before the long voyage ended, Cunard had made up his mind that he would take action himself. He would

raise enough money to build three or four large passenger
steamers, then he would go to Parry with a proposal. For
a fixed annual fee, depending on the cost of the steamers,
he would offer to carry the mails and dispatches between
England, Halifax and New York. But instead of stopping
briefly at Halifax and then going on to New York as the
sailing packets did, he would propose making Halifax
the terminal, with auxiliary steamers carrying the mail
to and from New York. Or perhaps, since he had no wish
to compete with the steamers already going to New York,
he might persuade the Admiralty to deliver the United
States mail to Boston. In any case, making Halifax the
terminal would assure that port's position as a depot for
British trade with the United States.

Then there was the Canadian mail. In summer it was
still carried overland through New Brunswick, in winter
overland from Boston. But a railroad was under construction from Boston to the Hudson. One day soon it would
reach Buffalo and the lake steamers. When that happened,
the Canadians would be sure to want their mail delivered
via Boston all year round—unless, in the meantime, someone provided a better way. Cunard decided that his proposal to the Admiralty would include an auxiliary service
from Halifax to Quebec as well, thus assuring that Canada
would be dependent on Halifax as an overseas port of
entry.

He thought that when he explained all this to his business associates in Halifax they would be eager to join him
in financing a company which would be called the Ocean
Steam Packet Company or some similar name. But when
he reached home he found that none of the merchants
cared to risk such an investment. In fact, one or two advised him to give up the idea himself. It was a poor time,
they suggested, for Cunard to be talking about so tremen-

dous an undertaking as putting an "ocean railroad" across the Atlantic, when certain of his business enterprises at home were less profitable than they had been, and his whalers, at least, were losing money.

He had two whalers in the South Pacific. Word had come back from New Zealand that the crew of the *Samuel Cunard* had deserted, and her captain, in a fit of drunken despondency, had jumped overboard and drowned. Cunard would be lucky if the ship got home at all. The *Rose* had been gone three years, and nothing had been heard from her.

During July, while Cunard was still trying to raise money in Halifax, the amount of mail carried by the Falmouth packets dropped considerably. It was quicker to send letters by the *Great Western*. This meant a reduction in the mail carried by Cunard's Boston and Bermuda packets. In August, even the important government dispatches for all the colonies were sent to New York by the steamer and redistributed from there. "This is a cause of mortification," the Halifax papers complained.

Cunard went to Boston, where he tried to interest merchants and shipowners in his proposed steamship company. He found them still convinced that the Atlantic steamer would never be anything but a novelty, impractical as well as dangerous. It would never replace sail for transocean shipping. American sailing packets were already the fastest and most famous in the world. Boston shipowners intended to compete for their share of the Atlantic trade by building ocean windjammers that were bigger, faster, and more luxurious than anything yet imagined. Cunard returned to Halifax empty-handed.

Around this time, in London, Sir Edward Parry wrote to a friend in Glasgow, shipowner George Burns, advising him that the Admiralty was thinking of turning the Atlantic packet service over to some private steamship company. Would Burns care to make a bid for the contract? Burns wrote back that he was not interested. He had a fleet of steam coasters running between Liverpool and Glasgow, was making a fortune on them and had no wish to take part in such a risky business as placing steamers on the Atlantic.

Cunard knew nothing of this. He thought it would be a year, at least, before the Admiralty considered making a change in the Atlantic post. It would take that long to establish public confidence in the ocean steamer.

On November 8, an advertisement appeared in the London *Times*: "Steam vessels required for conveying Her Majesty's Mails and Dispatches between England and Halifax, N. S., and also between England, Halifax, and New York." A long list of conditions and regulations regarding the submission of tenders followed. The service was to start the next April, with ships running once a month. The port of departure could be Bristol, Falmouth, Liverpool, or Southampton. All tenders were to be submitted to the Admiralty before December 15.

This issue of the *Times* reached Halifax on the December packet, two weeks after the time limit was up.

Cunard sent a hasty note off to his brother Joe, saying that he was leaving at once for England, and boarded the return packet. By the time he reached London the closing date for tenders would be almost two months in the past, but he still hoped to make a bid for the Atlantic mail contract. Common sense told him that none of the existing steamship companies could meet the Admiralty demand for service to start in April. It would take more than a year to get ships ready. And since no steamer had yet crossed the Atlantic in winter, he did not think that many shipowners would risk promising year-round service.

# 6

When Sam reached London he found that two companies had submitted tenders. The Great Western Company had offered to start a monthly service as soon as ships could be built, which would be a year and a half. The St. George Steam Packet Company offered to start at once, with coastal steamers it already owned. But Cunard had been right about the winter sailings. Neither company wanted to risk sending a steamer out against the January gales that sweep southeast from Labrador.

Sir Edward Parry—who recalled with pleasure the winter evenings he had spent in the Cunard home twenty years before—indicated that he was far from satisfied with the two offers received. The closing date for tenders had been extended. There was still time for Cunard to put in his bid.

Reasoning that it would be easier to borrow money after he had got the contract, Sam submitted his proposal at once. Disregarding the Admiralty request for once-a-month service to New York via Halifax, he offered "to convey the mails from a point in England to Halifax twice a month. Also to provide branch boats . . . to convey the mails to Boston and back to Halifax. Likewise to provide boats . . . to convey the mails from Pictou to Quebec and back" during the navigation season. For this service, which was to start on May 1, 1840, he asked £55,000 a year.

When Parry told him that the Admiralty "might be prepared to entertain a proposition of this kind," Cunard looked around for a good shipbuilder.

The East India Company recommended the Glasgow firm of Wood and Napier. Robert Napier, the head of the firm and the best marine engineer in Britain, had designed the engines for the *British Queen* and built the *Berenice* and the *London* for the East India Company.

Cunard did not approach Napier directly. From his G.M.A. office on Ludgate Hill he wrote to a friend in Glasgow, William Kidston, head of a mercantile firm with which he did business. Would Mr. Kidston approach Mr. Napier and ask him the probable cost of building one or two steamers? "I want a plain and comfortable boat," Cunard wrote, "not the least unnecessary expense for show." After an exchange of letters, he went to Glasgow and called on Napier at his home, Lancefield House.

Napier had some revolutionary ideas about how a steamer should be operated. He advocated placing a first-class engineer in charge of the engine room, with trained personnel under him. And he thought that every vessel should have a complete workshop, with tools and replacement parts in case of breakdowns. Most shipowners tried to run their steamers as they had run their sailing ships, not realizing that a different kind of crew was needed—

Robert Napier, the marine engineer who designed and built Cunard's first steamships.

men who worked below deck and knew more about oiling machinery than making sail.

Cunard always sized people up quickly. Within half an hour he had decided that the spare, forthright Scot, whose ideas he considered sound, was the man with whom he wanted to do business. He asked Napier to give him a price on three steamers of eight hundred tons each.

Napier was anxious to get the order. He quoted a rock-bottom price of £32,000 (roughly $140,000) for each ship. Cunard, the wily trader, admitted that this was "a fair and reasonable" price. However, if Napier would take £30,000, he could have the order then and there. Napier finally agreed.

But back in London, Parry, the spokesman for the Admiralty, thought the 800-ton ships were too small. If Cunard would increase the size to 960 tons, he said, the mail contract was as good as signed. Cunard returned to Glasgow, where he signed a formal agreement with Napier to purchase three steamers of 960 tons at £32,000 each.

"From the frank off hand manner in which he contracted with me, I have given him the vessels cheap," Napier told his friend at the East India Company.

As soon as the agreement was signed, on March 18, 1839, Cunard left on the mail coach for London. "The Admiralty and Treasury are highly pleased with the size of the boats," he wrote Napier. "I have given credit where it is due to you and Mr. Wood." Then, shrewdly capitalizing on the age-old rivalry between England and Scotland, he added, "You have no idea of the prejudices of some of our English builders. I have had several offers from Liverpool and this place; and when I have replied that I have contracted in Scotland they invariably say, 'you will neither have substantial work, nor completed in time.' The Admiralty agree with me that the boats will be as good as if built in this country, and I have assured them you will keep to time."

Napier needed no such spur. He was well aware that the building of the Atlantic steamers could make or break him. "I am certain that they will be very good and strong ships," he said.

George Burns, one of Samuel Cunard's principal partners.

Cunard's contract with the Admiralty was not signed for another six weeks, but he was told that his tender had been accepted. The signing was a mere formality which would be attended to as soon as the papers were drawn up.

Joe spent two weeks in London before catching the April packet back to Halifax. He would have given anything to be in his brother's shoes. Sam was doing business on such a grand scale—conferring with the heads of the Admiralty, the Lords of the Treasury, the postmaster general's department. By comparison, his own activities in the wilds of New Brunswick seemed rather tame. Above all, Joe admired the way Sam had ordered the steamers before he had raised the money to pay for them. This was the way Joe himself liked to do business.

When the contract was finally signed, on May 4, Sam went back to Glasgow, where Napier had promised to help him in his search for capital. Napier introduced him to James Donaldson, a wealthy Glasgow cotton broker, and also to George Burns—the same George Burns who had been offered the contract some months before and had refused it.

Cunard was a good salesman. "It was not long before I began to see some daylight through the scheme," Burns said later. "That day I invited Cunard to dine with me, and also David MacIver." MacIver, who lived in Liverpool, was Burns's partner in the City of Glasgow Steam Packet Company.

MacIver was more difficult to persuade. It was not until the next morning, when the three went out to Lancefield House to have breakfast with Napier that he agreed to risk some capital in Cunard's Atlantic steam venture. Burns, MacIver and Napier were so well known in Glasgow that it was not difficult to find other investors. A company was formed with thirty-four shareholders, and £270,000 was raised. Cunard put in £55,000; James Donaldson, £16,000; Napier, £6,000; Burns, £5,500; David MacIver and his brother Charles, £4,000 each. Other shareholders invested smaller amounts. The company was called the British and North American Royal Mail Steam Packet Company. Nobody could remember such a long name. From the beginning the newspapers and the general public substituted "Mr. Cunard's Company" or simply "Cunard's."

Sam Cunard was still in Glasgow when word came from Halifax that the whaler *Rose* had come home in early April with a full cargo. It seemed a good omen.

In March, he had written to friends in Boston giving a brief outline of his contract with the Admiralty. The letter reached Boston April 21. The next day a special meeting of the merchants was held in the Tremont Bank, where it was decided to write Cunard and ask him to persuade the Admiralty to extend the service and have the mail delivered to Boston by the Atlantic steamers instead of by branch boats from Halifax.

The letter, signed by the Boston merchants, was forwarded to Glasgow. The shareholders of the new steam packet company held a meeting, and decided that this would be a good move. There was now enough money in the treasury to build four ships instead of three and to make them larger.

Cunard was faced with a difficult decision. One reason he had gone after the mail contract in the first place was to assure that Halifax would be the terminal for the steamers, the depot for British trade with the United States, which would mean increased business for S. Cunard & Co. Now he had to look at the situation from the viewpoint of a British shipowner instead of a colonial merchant. He had to agree that Boston, grown to a city of 85,000 people, was the logical choice for the terminal. Halifax could not supply enough passengers and freight to make the line pay. Since the bulk of trade would be with Boston, it would be cheaper and more convenient to load the ships there. Regretfully, he sided with the majority. It was the first of a number of such decisions he would be forced to make in the years to come, with Halifax usually on the losing side.

The partners presented a new proposal to the Ad-

miralty. They would put four ships, up to twelve hundred
tons, with cabin space for 115 passengers, on the mail
run. The steamers would sail from Liverpool on the 4th
and 19th of each month, would stop briefly at Halifax to
deliver the mail, then go on to Boston, calling at Halifax
again on the way back to England. Liverpool was chosen
as the eastern terminal because, of the four points of departure named by the Admiralty, it was the closest to
Glasgow.

The Admiralty accepted the amended proposal. A new
contract was drawn up, the subsidy being increased to
£60,000. "I never liked the word subsidy," Burns complained. "It was freight paid for the carriage of letters."
The £60,000 was in fact less than the yearly cost of main-
taining the sailing packets had been. The new contract
was signed by Cunard, Burns and MacIver, the three
active partners in the steamship company.

In July, Cunard sailed for New York on the *Great
Western,* leaving David and Charles MacIver to super-
vise the building of the Liverpool terminal. The four
steamers were already under construction on the Clyde.


Joe Cunard had reached Halifax in late April. He stayed
long enough to tell everyone about the mail contract.
Though the Admiralty had not at that time accepted
Sam's tender, Joe intimated that it was all settled. The
service would start in about a year, he said, and Halifax
would be the terminal. His news threw the whole town
into a ferment of excitement. Halifax would be the only
port in America where ocean steamers arrived and de-
parted on schedule. And twice a month, too! Even New
York would be put in the shade.

"A new era will commence in provincial prosperity

from the moment the first steam packet reaches Halifax," one local paper reported, "and no one who knows the superior position of our port but must be convinced that the time is not far distant when it will become the center of steam navigation for the whole North American continent."

"Thousands will visit us in search of business or pleasure," another editor wrote. The merchants became so enthusiastic about the future of Halifax and the crowds of travelers who were expected to arrive on the steamers, that they called a special meeting and raised enough money to build a luxury hotel.

Well satisfied with the furor he had created in Halifax, Joe continued his journey to Miramichi. He had recently gone into shipbuilding, having bought existing yards at Chatham and built new ones at Bathurst on the shore of Baie Chaleur. In England, he had obtained orders for six ships, which would come off the ways before the year ended: the *Jane, Susan,* and *Caroline* at Bathurst, the *Ann, Margaret,* and *Joseph Cunard* on the Miramichi.

Instead of sailing direct to Miramichi, Joe stopped off at a small seaport on the New Brunswick coast and sent a messenger ahead to his town of Chatham with two news items: first, he now had enough orders to keep the shipyards and the timber gangs busy for another year, and second, the Cunards were about to start a line of steamers across the Atlantic with the British mail. There was no need to hint that Joe was mainly responsible for the mail contract. His people naturally jumped to that conclusion.

Joe gave them time to prepare a welcome, then he rode overland through the woods to Chatham. Signal fires on the hills announced his coming. A parade of horsemen galloped out to meet him and escort him back to town, where he was greeted with a salute of eighteen guns, church bells, a parade and a formal address of welcome. It was his most spectacular homecoming yet. The next night he was toasted at a public dinner where he was the principal speaker. Unlike Sam, Joe loved to make speeches.

By the time Sam reached home in late summer the terms of the amended contract had been made public, and though it was known that the steamers would go on to Boston, everyone kept on wishfully thinking of Halifax as the terminal. Sam's welcome home was not quite as spectacular as Joe's had been, but he was given a monster open-air reception where the whole town could applaud "the colonist . . . who had the courage to grapple with an undertaking so vast as the carriage of mail by steamer between Halifax and the Mother Country."

His children saw very little of him that year, he was so busy arranging port facilities in Boston, Halifax, Pictou and Quebec. In Boston, a site on recently reclaimed Noddle's Island was leased to the steamship company, rent free, for a period of twenty-eight years, and work on the docks began there in September. In Halifax, the largest of Cunard's three wharves at the foot of Proctor's Lane was made ready. The existing stagecoach service would be employed to carry the mails overland to Pictou, a hundred miles away, to connect with the auxiliary service up to Quebec. The *Unicorn*, a steam coaster built in Glasgow in 1836, had been purchased for this run.

In September, Cunard went to Pictou to arrange port facilities there, and a little later the family joined him at Mount Rundell for the opening of G.M.A.'s six-mile steam railroad from the Albion Mine to the dock. The rail line was not actually finished, but G.M.A. officials in London had become so impatient that it was decided to hold the grand opening anyway.

The *Samson* (in 1839), the first steam locomotive in the Atlantic provinces. Owned by the General Mining Association, and used to transport coal from the pithead of the Albion Mine to the docks at Pictou, six miles away. The *Samson*, housed at New Glasgow, Nova Scotia, is still in running order.

In May, three dismantled steam locomotives had been shipped out from Newcastle upon Tyne on the brig *Ytham*. They were named the *Samson*, the *Hercules* and the *John Buddle*. The *Samson*—the first steam locomotive ever seen in those parts—had been assembled and given a trial run. On opening day the *Samson* ran back and forth along the finished part of the line hauling a string of coal cars filled with mine officials and their children. Later on the miners and their families were given free rides.

At noon, at a barbecue luncheon in the formal garden at Mount Rundell, a whole steer roasted over a fire pit and casks of West India rum were placed on convenient sawhorses. In the evening, a dinner party was held in the new stone engine house where the locomotives were to be kept. The head table was decorated with a miniature railroad track along which a miniature train carried the wine decanters.

More toasts were drunk to Sam Cunard, the Steam Lion, the hero of the day, than to the men who had built the railroad. No one forgot that every time the Atlantic steamers stopped at Halifax, their bunkers would be filled with G.M.A. coal.

In February, 1840, the first of the Atlantic steamers was launched on the Clyde. The *Britannia* slid into the water without a hitch, but Cunard and his partners knew that she could never be made ready for sea by May 1, the date they had promised to begin service to America. The three vessels still on the stocks—to be named *Acadia*, *Caledonia* and *Columbia*—were months behind schedule, too. And the contract specified that the company would have to pay a fine of £1,000 for every departure "delayed twelve hours or more." At the rate things were going, the first year's fines would put the company in the red.

Cunard also realized by this time that it had been a mistake to promise twice-a-month service in winter. In summer, the four ships would be able to keep up this schedule, but winter voyages would take longer, and five ships would be needed. He was faced with the task of persuading the Admiralty to accept a revised winter schedule.

In London, he took this problem to Parry. From Piccadilly to Parry's house in Devonshire Place was a pleasant walk, and he went there often. Parry agreed that the winter schedule was impossible to keep up with the present fleet. He wrote to the Board of Admiralty, urging them to allow Cunard "the remission which he solicits—namely that his vessels shall proceed only once, instead of twice each month during November, December, January and February." He recommended that "no deduction be made from the amount of Mr. Cunard's contract."

The Admiralty agreed to a reduced winter service, but the fines for missed sailings in summer still held, and by the middle of April it was estimated that the *Britannia* would be two months behind schedule. The little steamer purchased for the St. Lawrence service was ready for delivery to Halifax, however. Ned, who was to be the company's representative at home, was to sail with her from Liverpool in May. It was decided that the *Unicorn* would be the first steamer of the line—already being referred to as the "Cunard Line"—to carry the mails to America.

On Saturday, May 16, Ned set out from Liverpool on the *Unicorn*. There were twenty-six other passengers. The steamer had a rough crossing, "nothing but gales of wind from the west and the northwest; it blew one night a perfect hurricane," Captain Douglas reported. But she passed Cape Race on the fourteenth day and on the morning of June 1 was sighted off Sambro Light.

Cunard's blue flag with its white star was hoisted on the signal staff on Citadel Hill, but the *Unicorn* was flying a new pennant: a blue streamer with a white St. Andrew's cross near the hoist and a narrow red streamer under it—the house flag of the British and North American Royal Mail Steam Packet Company.

Ned was king for a day in his home town. Although the big celebration was being saved for the *Britannia,* he was met by a party of civic officials who delivered speeches of welcome and led the cheering. People really did cheer in those days. When "Three cheers for Mr. Cunard!" was proposed, everybody screamed "Hurrah!" three times and followed it up with a tiger cheer. The *Unicorn* was the

Flag of the first Cunard steamship: a blue streamer with a white St. Andrew's cross near the hoist, and a narrow red streamer beneath it.

first transatlantic steamer ever to touch at Halifax. People surged through the narrow waterfront streets by the thousands for a glimpse of her.

Late that night the *Unicorn* steamed off to Boston. Half the passengers had disembarked at Halifax, but about a dozen members of the Cunard and Duffus families took advantage of all the spare cabins to share the excitement of the arrival at Boston. Margaret and Jane, Willie and the two youngest Cunard girls, Isabel and Elizabeth, were on board, the girls armed with a list of things to buy for Jane's wedding, which was to take place that autumn.

A bigger reception awaited the *Unicorn* in Boston. The revenue cutter *Hamilton* and the frigate *Columbus* were decked with flags and sent out to escort her up the bay, with bands playing. A flotilla of yachts and small sailboats from the fashionable summer colony of Nahant followed. British and American flags flew from special flagpoles erected all over the city. Church bells rang. Cannon salutes from shore batteries were so loud that "the handsome painted glass windows" of the *Unicorn's* saloon were shattered.

That night, Ned was the guest of honor at a banquet for 450 people put on by the city. His brother and sisters were not invited to this all-male affair, so they missed hearing the great poet Longfellow, who was the principal speaker.

Back in England, while the *Britannia* was being made ready at the Coburg Dock in Liverpool, Cunard and his partners were framing the "rules of management" that were to make the line famous for safety. Napier's idea of placing trained personnel in the engine room had been carried out. Each man under the chief engineer had a specific job to do and was thoroughly trained to do it. By putting safety above profit, the partners hoped to build up the confidence of the large section of the traveling public who still considered it "a risk of human life" to sail on the ocean steamers. Lookouts were to be on the job every minute, watching for derelicts, icebergs and other ships.

But certain safety measures recommended by Parry were not put into effect for many years. Parry urged "the carrying of particular lights, arranged in one uniform manner, whereby *at first sight*, every seaman shall be able to say in what direction a vessel is going" and "the adoption of one uniform 'rule of the road'—leaving no doubt . . . on which side vessels are to pass one another." Such precautions were not considered necessary on the open ocean, where other ships were not often sighted. Running lights were unheard of. Sometimes a lantern was hung in the bowsprit when another ship was sighted at sea, but at the approach to harbor a light was the signal that a pilot was needed.

The *Britannia* was 207 feet long, a two-decker with one tall red funnel amidships and huge paddle wheels. She had a square stern, a clipper bow and a bronze figurehead —Britannia carrying a trident—under the bowsprit. On the upper deck were the officers' quarters, the galley, bakery, and the cowhouse. Cows were carried to supply fresh milk. The rest of the deck was open, a working space where all the gear for sails and yards was stored, more like the deck of a sailing ship than a modern steamer. *Britannia* was bark-rigged: fore-and-aft rigged on the mizzenmast, square-rigged on the mainmast and foremast. The ship had three furnaces, carried six hundred tons of coal, and was steered by hand. The wheel was manned by from four to six sailors, depending on the weather. These men had the hardest jobs on the ship, and the most dangerous. In heavy seas a sailor could be badly injured if the wheel "threw him off."

The passenger cabins and dining saloon were on the second deck. The saloon contained no luxury items, though it was described as "tastefully furnished." The cabins, each accommodating two persons, were eight by six feet. Each had two bunks, one above the other, one thinly upholstered settee and a commode with two set-in washbasins, two water jugs and two chamber pots. Four hooks were provided on which to hang clothes. The only light was a hurricane candle beside the porthole. The corridors were lit by candles suspended in trays. These feeble flickering lights were extinguished at ten o'clock each night to cut down the fire hazard.

A printed list of "rules and regulations" posted in each cabin informed the passengers that their bed linen would be changed on the eighth day of the voyage, two towels would be provided for each passenger and changed "every other day or as often as required," the staterooms would be swept and the carpets taken out and shaken every morning after breakfast, and smoking below deck was strictly forbidden.

Since sending mail overseas was expensive—the ship letter rate was one shilling for a single sheet, two shillings for a double—every transatlantic traveler had his pockets and luggage stuffed with "home letters" handed to him by friends, which he either delivered by hand or sent on by post at the end of the voyage. The amount of mail carried by passengers represented such a loss of revenue that Cunard, an old carrier of home letters himself, had notices printed and prominently displayed on all the ships, demanding that "all gentlemen having letters" hand them over to the mail officer "to be put into a bag."

The *Britannia*'s maiden voyage was scheduled for Saturday, July 4, 1840. On Friday the heavy luggage was put on board at the Coburg Dock, then the steamer was swung out into the Mersey. "Owing to her immense size," she could only be got away from the dock at high tide. The passengers and mail went aboard the next morning from a tender.

At six that evening the *Britannia* set out for America. She carried ninety-three crew members and sixty passengers including Cunard, his daughter Ann and her friend Laura Haliburton, a tall attractive girl of sixteen who showed promise as an artist. The girls had been staying with Mrs. Haliburton's people, the Nevilles, who lived near Bristol. The weather was good, the voyage was smooth and uneventful. The steamer reached Halifax twelve and a half days later.

The *Britannia* leaving Liverpool, July 4, 1840.

Halifax, in the midst of preparing a civic reception, was literally caught napping. There was no way of knowing when the steamer would arrive. The *Unicorn,* still in port, had taken sixteen days. The *Britannia* was expected to make slightly better time—perhaps fourteen days.

Before dawn on the thirteenth day, a cannon shot aroused the sleeping town. This was the signal agreed on if the *Britannia* arrived after dark. Officials of the welcome committee tumbled out of bed and rushed about to get the reception started. The speeches had been written and rehearsed, but it took some time to round up the committee and issue final instructions. An hour later the delegation hurried down to Cunard's Wharf, where the *Britannia* lay, her bronze figurehead gleaming in the early light. Already the Long Wharf was jammed with people, some lining up at the foot of the gangplank for an inspection tour of the ship. Trunks and boxes were being loaded onto drays, officers were handing up the letterbags. But in this scene of confusion there was no sign of Sam Cunard.

What had happened, the committee learned later, was that the steamer had been berthed for some time before the cannon shot sounded because nobody had remembered to inform the signalman of her arrival. Cunard's family had been on the lookout, however, and were waiting on the dock when the vessel tied up. They had been taken on a tour of the ship and had all gone home to breakfast.

The chief topic of conversation at home was nineteen-year-old Jane's engagement to Captain Gilbert Francklyn of the 37th Regiment. The match had been approved by Grandmother Duffus. Cunard had given his consent to the engagement by letter, and the wedding was to take place in September. A servant was sent running to find Captain

Francklyn, who was thirty years old and unfortunately had no property—"but he seems to be a very good young man," Cunard conceded—and fetch him back to meet his future father-in-law.

At seven, a group of civic officials arrived to formally congratulate the town's most distinguished native son. But the speeches were only half finished when a message came from Captain Woodruff: the cargo consigned to Halifax had been taken off the *Britannia,* her coal supply had been replenished, pilot John Fitzgerald was on board, and the steamer would sail in half an hour.

The plans for a public reception had to be shelved for the time being. There was only enough time to get a few ships decked with flags to escort the *Britannia* out past the lighthouse. She sailed at nine o'clock that morning, leaving everybody in Halifax feeling a bit deflated. She had come and gone so quickly. The Falmouth packets had never been in such a hurry.

By noon, the *Unicorn* had got under way for Quebec with the Canadian mail. On the return voyage she would dock at Pictou, and subsequent sailings would be made from that port. In midafternoon, when the tide turned, Cunard's mail brig *Lady Paget* left for Bermuda, and another sailing packet, not Cunard's, set out for Newfoundland. There had been no mail service between Halifax and Newfoundland before 1840. Letters had been entrusted to the trader captains who could charge what they liked for delivery. That summer a government-subsidized packet service was started with two little schooners, the *Sandwich* and the *Charles Buchan,* leaving twice a month for St. John's.

The *Britannia* reached Boston at ten o'clock the next night, Saturday. Her arrival was announced by the band of the frigate *Columbus* playing "God Save the Queen"—

the signal for people to "come running from their homes" to watch the wonderful new ocean steamer dock.

Boston had plenty of time to stage an official reception. A committee had been set up to plan various public ceremonies to "welcome the Britannia to our waters." Five thousand dollars had been raised by public subscription, and a silver loving cup two and a half feet high was ready for presentation to the founder of the new packet line. Tuesday was proclaimed "Cunard Festival Day." A parade of citizens marching eight abreast was headed by government and civic leaders of all the New England states. This was climaxed by a dinner for 2,300 people held in a temporary pavilion in front of the Maverick House Hotel and presided over by the governor of Massachusetts. Josiah Quincy, president of Harvard College, proposed the first toast—"Health, happiness and prosperity to Mr. Cunard." Daniel Webster of New Hampshire, America's foremost orator, was the principal speaker.

To everyone's relief, after Webster's eloquent but overlong address, Cunard made his speech of thanks brief and to the point. He was, he said, "altogether unused to speechmaking" and could never find language to express his heartfelt gratification at the reception he had been given.

The New England papers were full of news of Mr. Cunard and the *Britannia*. All other news was crowded off the front pages. "Never since the arrival of the Pilgrim Fathers have the shores of America experienced so important an event," one journalist wrote. (In Halifax, Judge Haliburton had gone one better: "Since the discovery of America by Columbus, nothing has occurred of so much importance to the new world as navigating the Atlantic by steamers.")

The *Britannia* left Boston on August 3. She steamed into

Halifax the next day, paused long enough to pick up the mail and a few passengers, then sailed off to Liverpool, leaving Sam Cunard behind to await the arrival of the *Acadia,* due to leave Liverpool on the same day.

Halifax could not hope to match the grand reception Cunard had received in Boston, but the welcome committee did its best. At a public meeting the local boy who had made good was presented with a scroll signed by several thousand people. If there was general disappointment because the *Britannia* had stayed two weeks in Boston and only a few hours in Halifax, it was gamely suppressed for the time being.

# 7

All four ships of the Cunard fleet were in service by the end of January, 1841. The *Columbia* made her first voyage from Liverpool to Halifax, against the icy winds and rough seas of midwinter, in less than fourteen days.

Boston and Halifax were now the only two American ports with a regular year-round steamer service to and from Europe. Four ocean steamers made occasional calls at New York: the *British Queen,* her sister ship the new *President,* the *Liverpool* and the *Great Western.* But these ships had no set schedule.

New Yorkers, unwilling to concede that Boston was now ahead of them, talked about the superiority of their sailing packets, the fastest and most luxurious in the world. The ships of the Black Ball, Dramatic, Star, Swallow Tail and other packet lines were always booked to capacity. Since many people still thought that crossing the Atlantic by steamer was so risky as to be almost suicidal, the steamers often carried more crew than passengers. "There is to be something of a contest between our far-famed sailing packets and the steamers," James Gordon Bennett's New York *Herald* predicted early in 1841. "It is yet to be discovered which are the most comfortable and profitable."

But Bennett was quick to see the value of the Cunard steamers for regular delivery of overseas news to fill the columns of his *Herald,* for the steamers were the fastest and most reliable carriers of overseas dispatches. The *Unicorn* had made it possible for Boston newspapers to print the ghoulish details of Lord William Russell's murder (he was found in bed with his throat slashed) two days before New York got the story. The *Britannia* brought a report about an attempt on Queen Victoria's life. When Dickens' *The Old Curiosity Shop* was running serially in a London weekly, Halifax and Boston readers, on edge with anxiety over literature's most long-suffering child, waited on the dock for news of Little Nell.

In order to bring dispatches quickly to his newspaper, Bennett stationed America's first foreign correspondent in Halifax. Bennett's man boarded the Cunard steamers at Halifax, culled the news from the British periodicals while enroute to Boston, then rushed it by pony express to New York. There was no direct rail line between the two cities, though Boston was linked to the Hudson by the new Western Railroad.

The disappearance of the *President* in March, 1841, almost spelled disaster for all the Atlantic steamers, as a great new section of the public joined the anti-steam faction. The *President* left New York for Liverpool in fair weather, with a total of 136 passengers and crew. She was sighted a few days later near the Grand Banks, in heavy seas, and was never seen again. The loss ruined her London owners. They withdrew the *British Queen* from the Atlantic service and sold her on the continent.

The owners of the *Liverpool* soon found that they were losing money on the Atlantic run. They went out of business, and sold their steamers to the P. & O. Company, then running a line of mail boats to Gibraltar and Alexandria. Cunard's competition was reduced to one steamer, the *Great Western*—and the sailing packets with their elegantly appointed spacious cabins. Cunard and his partners made no attempt to provide the same luxurious accommodation on the steamers. Their main concern was to build up a reputation for safety, and they went to extreme lengths to cut down the possibility of accidents.

Two months after the *President* disappeared, the *Britannia* struck a reef off Sambro Light in a dense fog. She was inbound from Boston and had been taken over by the Halifax pilot when she struck. She was backed off the reef and taken to Cunard's Wharf, where the passengers were put ashore. The damage was slight, the ship was not leaking. But the *President* disaster was fresh in the passengers' minds. To reassure them, the *Britannia* was sent around to Saint John for a more thorough examination. Only when she had been checked from stern to bowsprit was she allowed to return to Halifax and pick up her passengers.

Sam was in London, successfully working out a renewal of his contract with the Admiralty. He had turned the management of S. Cunard & Co. of Halifax over to his brother Edward. The G.M.A. agency was the only branch of his colonial business that he still handled himself. This was a job that entailed an enormous amount of correspondence with coal dealers in the United States. All through the early years of the steamship line, Cunard's income as North American distributor for G.M.A. coal was greater than the return from his investment in ocean steamers.

Cunard signed another contract that year, one that was sharply criticized back home in Nova Scotia. Colonel Maberley, the secretary general of the British Post Office, offered him a subsidy of £1,550 a year to transport the Canadian mail by coach from the Cunard steamers at Halifax to the *Unicorn* which ran between Pictou and Quebec. Nobody else was offered a chance to bid on this contract, which Cunard signed in London.

The existing stagecoach service was discontinued, and Cunard's put a fleet of fast four-horse coaches on the road between Pictou and Halifax. The hundred-mile drive took two days. Horses were stabled every ten miles along the way. In spring, the roads were so bad that the horses often floundered in mud up to their knees. A dozen times a day the passengers had to be taken off, while teams of oxen from nearby farms hauled the coach to drier ground.

At the time the contract was signed, the colonial mail service was under the jurisdiction of the British Post Office. A change was made that year, and each province was allowed to handle its own postal affairs. But the contract between Cunard and the British Post Office was still valid, and the Nova Scotia government had to foot the bill for a service it considered quite unnecessary. The old stagecoaches had done the job well enough and for a lot less money. The government of Canada, which had been expected to pay half the subsidy, refused to contribute anything. The Cunard coaches ran three times a week, but delivered mail to the *Unicorn* only twice a month. Canada had no intention of subsidizing what was in reality a profitable passenger service.

The furor over the coach contract came at an awkward time. The local newspapers were complaining—rather belatedly—that Halifax was regarded "merely as the *touching* place for the Cunard steamers, while Boston was selected as the *stopping* place." The elegant new Halifax Hotel, built to accommodate the flood of visitors the steamers were expected to bring, stood empty. The visitors had all gone on to Boston. Sam Cunard was not such a hero in his home town as he had been the year before.

Joe's activities were criticized from time to time, too. Joe was a hero in his own town, but his arrogant lordliness was often resented in other places. There had been a public protest in Prince Edward Island about his handling of the mail contract he had bought from S. Cunard & Co. Some time after this had blown over, and "Mr. Cunard's assurance that such irregularities would not occur again" had been accepted, a Halifax newspaper published an open letter to the merchants warning them that Joe was a poor credit risk, as he owed money everywhere.

Ned Cunard, who took himself and his responsibilities rather seriously, attempted to defend his uncle. He wrote the newspaper: "My father being absent, I feel it my duty to deny most positively the slanderous and false assertions and insinuations contained in that letter respecting the amount of notes issued by Joseph Cunard & Company. The sum at present does not exceed four thousand pounds and never at any time amounted to more than one eighth of that stated." But he was wrong, the newspaper had not exaggerated. Joe was more deeply in debt than any of his family realized.

A little later, Joe lost the mail contract altogether, and at the same time Henry resigned as manager of Joseph

Cunard & Co. A story reached Halifax that the brothers
had disagreed over Joe's slapdash and often ruthless business methods. Hadn't Joe once said that he didn't care
how much money he lost as long as he had more "deals"
going than his competitors? And wasn't it true that a
farmer delivering produce to the company store could
collect payment a dozen times, by presenting his bill to
one clerk after another?

The gossip soon died down. Henry, it appeared, had
simply got tired of the businessman's life. He had retired—
at thirty-seven—to Woodburn, his country place on the
Miramichi, where he raised crops and cattle and organized agricultural meetings and plowing matches.

Joe's empire appeared to be as prosperous as ever. Few
people guessed that all through the year 1842 he was
teetering on the edge of bankruptcy. Joe managed to
keep his money troubles from Sam, who was too busy with
steamship matters to keep an eye on all the happenings
at home. Joe made a good job of appearing more successful than he was. He tore up the harshly-worded letters
from creditors, juggled funds from one branch of his company to another and kept on borrowing, sure that the next
day or the next his luck would change.

Joe's luck did change, because business conditions took
a sudden upswing, and because certain firms in Quebec
and Miramichi saw that the only way to save themselves
was to save Joe and "keep his various establishments in
motion." By the end of the year he had weathered the
slump and had more deals working than ever before.

A few murmurs of discontent over the coach contract
had reached Sam's ears, but he thought that those who
complained were simply opposed to progress. The coaches

had been running for six months before he had a chance
to test the service himself. In the summer of 1842, a week
after his return from England, he boarded the coach for
Mount Rundell and a conference with Richard Smith at
the Albion Mine.

Bowling along in fine weather over the dry summer
roads, he thought only that the new coaches were a vast
improvement over the old ones. No doubt, too, he was
conscious of his role as a benefactor, having provided
such excellent transportation between the two chief towns
of the province.

He was looking forward, that summer, to the birth of
his first grandchild. Jane's daughter, Margaret, was born
in October. In December, just before he left again for
London, Cunard saw the whaler *Rose* off on her second
Pacific cruise.

By the end of that year, too, the strict attention to
safety aboard the Cunard steamers was beginning to pay
off. More and more travelers discarded their fears of
engine failures and exploding boilers, though some complained that the accommodations were less comfortable
than on the sailing packets. When Dickens visited Joseph
Howe at the beginning of his American lecture tour,
he did nothing but grumble about the discomforts he had
endured on the *Britannia*. At the end of the tour, he sailed
for home on the Swallow Tail packet *George Washington*.

"Cunard's steamers will have to come direct from Liverpool to New York or they will be run off the ocean by the
New York packet ships in less than two years," Bennett
of the *Herald* warned. "They cannot get passengers at
Boston. People will not go so far out of their way."

The truth was, and Bennett knew it, that by this time
people were going to Boston in droves to sail on the

steamers, and the city was prospering as a result. The population of Boston increased from 85,000 in 1840 to 114,000 in 1845. The steamers contributed greatly to this expansion, though for every steamer that arrived in Boston there were more than a hundred sailing ships. The fabulous era of the clippers was just beginning. Donald McKay, the most famous American shipbuilder, launched his first clipper in 1846.

The steamers had also helped to introduce English plants to American gardens and had provided the Royal Botanical Gardens at Kew with many American plants. Cunard had met Sir William Hooker, the newly appointed director of Kew Gardens, at the home of Sir Edward Parry. Hooker had edited the *Botany of Parry's Third Voyage,* published in 1826. This was the age when British botanists were scouring the world for the seeds of strange plants. During a discussion one evening at Parry's new home in Hampstead, Hooker told of his attempts to bring live plants from New York on the sailing packets. The voyage had taken too long, and the plants had died. Cunard, who was keenly interested in horticulture, urged him to try the steamers.

Special glass-covered containers were provided, and in the spring of 1843 the first shipment of live plants from Kew Gardens was delivered in good condition to the Boston Botanical Gardens. This was the beginning of a regular exchange between the two countries. For his interest in this project, Cunard was elected a Fellow of the Royal Geographical Society.

In the summer of 1843, when the steamship company had been operating exactly three years, what was to prove one of the worst accidents in the history of the line occurred.

Cunard was in Halifax, awaiting the arrival of the *Columbia*. She had been scheduled to leave Boston on Saturday, July 1, under the command of Captain Neil Shannon, "a fine Scotch sailor with good stories," and should have reached Halifax on Monday morning. But all day Monday passed and there was no sign of her. The whole town waited uneasily. People gathered in knots on the streets to discuss possible causes of the delay. Tuesday passed, and apprehension grew. Then, early on Tuesday evening, the brig *Acadia* raced into port with the news. The *Columbia* was aground on a rock near Seal Island.

She had been twenty-five hours out of Boston, in thick fog, steering a course that should have taken her thirty miles south of Seal Island, when she struck a reef called the Devil's Limb. At certain seasons, the ocean current that slips past Seal Island from the northeast is deflected by a stronger current pushing up from the south. Three schooners from Boston, steering the same course as the mail steamer, had been carried off course by the variable current and did not know where they were until they heard the *Columbia*'s distress guns and went to investigate. The guns also brought the keeper of the Seal Island light.

Except for the fog, the weather was good. The sea was calm, and the eighty-five passengers on the *Columbia* were in no great danger. The steamer could not sink. She could only settle more firmly on the reef, stuck there like a broken eggshell.

With the help of the lightkeeper, the passengers were taken ashore. The only buildings on the island were two houses, some barns and the hexagonal tower that the Lighthouse Commission under Cunard had put up twelve years before. But with bedding and food from the *Colum-*

*bia* the passengers were made comfortable while Captain Shannon and his crew transferred the mail and all other movables ashore.

It was Wednesday evening before Cunard arrived on the *Margaret,* a steamer owned by S. Cunard & Co. On Friday the shipwrecked passengers were safely delivered to Halifax. On Sunday they sailed for Liverpool on the *Margaret.*

Part of the *Columbia*'s crew stayed with her to salvage what they could before she broke up in the first storm. The ship was a complete loss, but three schooner loads of timber, machinery and other salvaged material was transported to Halifax. In a month, nothing was left to mark the spot where she had struck.

The New York *Herald* was quick to point out that if the *Columbia* had been sailing from New York to Liverpool, she could have avoided "the 450 miles of rock, ledge, shoals and fog" along the Nova Scotia coast.

But the fact was that the disaster did not damage the steamship line's reputation for safety. In a day when wrecks caused by the forces of nature were thought to be inevitable—as opposed to mechanical failures, which could be avoided—Captain Shannon's handling of the situation became almost a model of how to conduct a shipwreck. No person had been killed, injured or even forced to suffer much discomfort. Not one piece of mail or cargo had been lost.

A new steamer, the *Hibernia,* soon replaced the lost *Columbia.*

Six months later New Yorkers got another chance to say that Boston was second-rate as a terminal for the Atlantic steamers. In the winter of 1844, for the first time in memory, Boston harbor froze over. It began with a thin skim.

As the cold weather continued, each succeeding high tide flooded the frozen surface and added another layer until the whole area from Deer Island to the docks was strong enough to support sleighing parties and iceboats. Cargoes had to be transported in horse-drawn sledges to the limit of the ice sheet where the schooners waited. The ice out there was two feet thick. At the dock where the *Britannia* was tied up it was seven feet thick. The *Britannia* was trapped. New Yorkers on board reminded anyone who would listen that New York harbor *never* froze over.

All Boston knew what the New York papers would say. The *Herald*'s correspondent was working the pony express overtime, speeding dispatches about the *Britannia*'s plight to the rival city. Boston was losing face, and something had to be done. The merchants got together and raised enough money to cut a seven-mile channel from the Cunard docks to the edge of the ice sheet. A gang of fifty men sawed the ice into square cakes one hundred feet across. A group of men stood on each cake, depressing one side of it with their weight until others, with grappling hooks and peaveys, could slide it under the edge of the main sheet. Then horses and men working together hauled the giant cakes away under the ice to the sides of the channel.

Two days later the *Britannia* was free. Jubilant Bostonians turned out to escort her down the channel to the sea. Sleigh bells jingled, skaters raced alongside, iceboats skimmed back and forth. The steamer was only three days behind schedule.

The rail line from Albany to Buffalo was finished that year, which meant that the Canadian mail could be carried swiftly from the Cunard steamers at Boston to the

Great Lakes steamers at Buffalo. Canada demanded that its overseas mail be sent that way. The dispute between Canada and Nova Scotia over Canada's refusal to pay half the cost of Cunard's Halifax–Pictou coach service had gone on so long that an official had been sent out from England to settle it.

Cunard himself was now anxious to terminate this contract, as well as the steamer service to Quebec. European travelers enroute to Canada no longer disembarked at Halifax, to endure the two-day coach ride to Pictou and there board the *Unicorn* for the long voyage to the St. Lawrence. It was so much quicker and more comfortable to disembark at Boston and take the railroad up to the Lakes. The *Unicorn* was losing money.

Besides, Cunard had signed a contract to carry the mails between Halifax and St. John's, Newfoundland. He wanted to transfer the *Unicorn* to that run.

In London, Cunard had been asked to accompany an official of the British Post Office to Washington to see what could be done about arranging a permanent agreement with the U. S. Postmaster General that would allow the Canadian mails to be transported over United States territory without examination or duty. It was largely through Cunard's "personal exertions," according to the Halifax papers, that such an agreement was signed in 1845.

The Canadian mail was no longer put ashore at Halifax. Cunard's fleet of four-horse coaches was sold. The *Unicorn* was taken off the Quebec run and transferred to the Newfoundland service.

Joseph Howe vigorously opposed this move, which made Canada independent of Halifax as a depot for overseas mail. Ten years later Howe was still making impassioned speeches about the injustice of "ocean steamers carrying British mail past British provinces to reach their destination through a foreign state."

But Howe did not blame his friend Cunard. He blamed Britain's colonial policy, which gave the provinces so little voice in their own affairs, and—more to the point—the changing pattern of transportation, the growing importance of the railroad in the development of any country and the fact that Halifax had no overland communication with the interior. Howe and Cunard were both aware that the rapid growth of New York since the 1820's was due, first, to the ease with which freight could be transported up the Hudson and along the Erie Canal to the Great Lakes and on to the Midwest, and, second, to the railroads pushing overland.

Many public meetings had been held in Halifax to discuss the need for a railroad up to Canada, but a survey had shown that the cost of laying tracks from Halifax up through the wilds of New Brunswick to Quebec would be very great. Cunard had always been a staunch advocate of the railroad, and when he withdrew the *Unicorn* from service he softened the blow by reporting to his friends back home that he and a number of London associates had got together and formed a company which proposed to build the Halifax to Quebec railroad—provided they could get the British government to put up the money.

This was good news. Everyone agreed that an extension of Cunard's "ocean railroad" would put Halifax back on the map. Goods, passengers and mail consigned to Canada would land at Halifax and go on to Quebec by train. Howe spoke optimistically about the hordes of immigrants who would follow the railroad, building towns in the wilderness.

Cunard had more than a philanthropic interest in the railroad. The land settlement company which he and Joe had set up controlled vast tracts of land in New Brunswick, much of it along the route of the proposed line. Once the tracks were laid and the country opened up, the Cunard brothers hoped to clean up a fortune selling lots to settlers.

But two years went by, and the British government was still undecided about providing funds. In 1847, when the House of Lords set up a special committee "to consider the subject of emigration from Ireland to the Colonies," it was suggested that the government be asked to put up the money for the Halifax to Quebec railroad and that the Irish be sent out to build it.

Because he was a shareholder in the railroad company and was familiar with conditions in the colonies, Cunard was invited to appear before the committee and give his opinion of this suggestion. Did he think the population of the Atlantic provinces was large enough to warrant the expense of a railroad?

Cunard made the most of his opportunity. The country was sparsely settled, he agreed, but he urged that the railroad be started immediately, as a means of getting immigrants into the interior. "I think you must settle the country as you go along," he said.

This seemed to the committee like putting the cart before the horse. They imagined a pathless wilderness of forest and marsh and mountains—which was in fact a fairly accurate picture. Would the train have to run some hundreds of miles through wild unsettled country? Would there be bears and wild animals?

Yes, the tracks would have to be laid through many miles of uninhabited territory, Cunard told them. "But it is fine fertile country, and will soon be settled." There was less danger from bears in the wilderness than from cattle in the settlements straying onto the tracks.

He was asked about mountains, and he told the committee about the line that was being built from Philadelphia to Pittsburgh over the Alleghenies, which were higher than the hills of New Brunswick. He told how America was pushing the iron tracks overland, providing transportation into the unsettled plains and forests of the interior, and how settlers were following the railroads into the wilderness and building towns there. Without railroads, the British colonies in North America could never hope to utilize all their natural resources.

The committee listened gravely, made notes, and retired to think it over. A transcript of the meeting was placed in a leather folder for safekeeping, then forgotten. A few years later Joseph Howe took up the campaign to get the railroad started. But it was not started in Cunard's lifetime, and Howe was dead before it was finished.

# 8

At last, in the summer of 1846, the New York *Herald* could announce that the Cunard Line had seen the error of its ways and was preparing to extend its Atlantic service to New York. Under the terms of a new contract with the British Admiralty, Mr. Cunard planned to add four more steamers to his fleet and provide once-a-week service to America, with ships sailing alternately to Boston and New York.

The Great Western Company had made an unsuccessful bid for the carriage of the New York mails. Their "line" of ships consisted of two steamers, the *Great Western* and a revolutionary new iron steamer with a screw propeller instead of paddle wheels called the *Great Britain*. To the surprise of many, the great iron ship actually did float. But in September, 1846, two months after the Great Western Company's bid for part of the Atlantic mail contract had been rejected, the *Great Britain* rammed into the Irish coast, a good thirty miles off course. She was refloated some months later and put into service again, but her career as an Atlantic liner was finished. Discouraged, her owners decided to give up trying to compete with the Cunard Line. They withdrew the *Great Western* from the New York run and sold her to the West India packet service.

Four new steamers were ordered for Cunard's New York service, which was to begin on January 1, 1848. They were to be equipped with the running lights Parry had recommended back in 1840, white on the foremast, green on the starboard side and red on the port side.

Edward, who was to be the company's New York representative, assisted his father in arranging port facilities on the Jersey shore opposite the Battery. Ned had always wanted to take a more prominent part in steamship affairs. He had felt left out of things, stuck in Halifax, and at one time had talked his father into letting him take over the Boston office from Mr. Lewis, the agent there. But wise outspoken David MacIver had persuaded Sam that such a move would be, to use his word, impolitic. "It is removing the *only* existing link that gives the U. S. folks any connection with steamboat matters in this country," he wrote from Liverpool.

David MacIver had died since then, and his place in the firm had been taken over by his brother Charles. The three active partners—Cunard, Burns and MacIver—were quietly buying up all the original shares of the British and North American Royal Mail Steam Packet Company and would in a few years buy out all the shareholders.

At home in Halifax, William and his cousin John Morrow, both in their early twenties, took over the management of S. Cunard & Co. Sam spent about five months of each year in Halifax. His brother Edward, who had worked so efficiently behind the scenes for twenty-five years, had been forced to retire because of ill health. John, the shipmaster, had died in the spring of 1844, and a year later the dignified old patriarch William Duffus died at eighty-three.

Margaret and Ann were married, both living in England. Margaret's husband, William Mellish, was a Nottingham squire with an estate near Blyth. Ann had followed Jane's example and married an army captain, Ralph Allen, whose regiment had since been returned to England. Only the two youngest girls, Isabel and Elizabeth, were still at home.

Perhaps it was the death of his brother and the thought that he himself was nearing sixty that made Sam Cunard realize how little he had seen of his family during the past five years. He decided to give up his suite at the Burlington Hotel in London and take a house somewhere in the West End, where Isabel and Elizabeth could live with him during the winter months. But the death of Mr. Duffus had forced him to give up this idea. The girls, then aged seventeen and eighteen, had told him that they could not leave Grandmother Duffus at such a time.

The fact was that they had never particularly enjoyed being in London. They missed the crowded cheerful family life at home, and their father was always so busy with important people. He was really more like a kind uncle— a devoted uncle who came home after long months of grand achievement in the world of international business, laden with presents, to visit for a little while and vanish again into his own world.

His children were all intensely proud of him. He was fast becoming England's most prominent merchant prince, commanding respect and admiration everywhere. "Not infrequently," as the Halifax papers put it, he was "the trusted counselor and adviser of the highest in the land on

Thomas Chandler Haliburton (1796–1865). Judge of the Supreme Court of Nova Scotia, and noted humorist and historian, Haliburton was the creator of the popular character named "Sam Slick," a Yankee peddler of clocks ($40—marked up from $6.50) who appeared in *The Clockmaker, The Attaché,* etc. Haliburton's more serious works include *Rule and Misrule of the British in North America.* He was a British member of Parliament (Conservative) for the Cornwall riding of Launceton from 1859 to 1865.

important questions pertaining to maritime affairs," meaning that he had been received by the queen and Prince Albert and had talked to them about the effect of improved ocean navigation on the growth of the British empire.

Though his name was recognized everywhere in England and America, Sam Cunard was not the most celebrated Nova Scotian of his time. That distinction belonged to Judge Thomas Haliburton, while Joseph Howe was the local celebrity. Haliburton's *Letterbag of the Great Western, The Attaché, The Old Judge* and other books had made him the most popular humorous writer—next to Dickens—in the English-speaking world.

As his fame increased, Haliburton became more and more dissatisfied with the narrow life of the colonies. He sent his eight children to English schools and hoped when they were off his hands to make his home in London. In the meantime, the royalties from his books enabled him to retire from his position as Judge of the Supreme Court and devote his whole time to writing, living in what Nova Scotia considered fairly grand style. His children, like Cunard's, were rapidly growing up, marrying and moving away from home. Two of Haliburton's boys were destined to attain distinction in later life. Robert became a noted scientist, and Arthur, the youngest, was created Baron Haliburton of Windsor.

Always somewhat opinionated, Judge Haliburton had grown less tolerant since his wife's death in 1840. He was at loggerheads, temporarily, with Joseph Howe, whose efforts to establish responsible government in Nova Scotia he derided as "an attempt to adapt the machinery of a large empire to a small colony."

In his younger days Haliburton had himself been inter-

Joseph Howe (1804–1873). Son of John Howe, Postmaster General and King's Printer for the Atlantic Colonies and Bermuda, Joseph Howe, in 1848, gained "responsible government" for Nova Scotia. He was the owner and editor of the best newspaper in the colonies: *The Colonial Herald,* better known by its alternate title, *The Novascotian.*

ested in the reform movement—a folly he hoped everyone had forgotten. He was impatient with Cunard for continuing to treat Howe as a friend, when it was obvious that aside from his determination to ruin the country with his fanatical ideas about government, Howe was behind the campaign that was shaping up against one of Cunard's best sources of income in Nova Scotia—the General Mining Association. Howe, he felt, was feeding the people a lot of radical ideas, so that those who had cheered loudest when big business had moved in with up-to-date machinery and cash wages now grumbled about "monopolies."

Howe was actually winning his battle for responsible government. Stumping up and down the country fighting for the people's rights, charming young and old with his robust good looks and his sometimes robust wit, kissing the mothers as well as the babies, he campaigned against the crown-appointed governor, Lord Falkland, and his self-appointed council. Up in Canada there was bloodshed and rebellion as less able reformers tried to achieve by force what Howe did with words. He had the crowds screaming with laughter one minute, tense with anger the next. He could move an audience to tears and often did. "The grandiloquent language of a rural politician," Haliburton called it, but Howe was the people's hero. His salty witticisms became legend, and in the end it was laughter that swept Lord Falkland and his council out of office.

Cunard was sorry to see the old Tory regime upset, but he could not agree that the change was as revolutionary as the reformers claimed it was. No matter who held the reins of government in Nova Scotia, most colonial affairs were still decided in the British houses of parliament. But Howe planned to change that state of affairs, too, by persuading the British government to accept a member of parliament for the Atlantic provinces in the House of Commons.

Well pleased with the success of his reform movement, Howe turned his attention to a campaign to get the new electric telegraph extended to Halifax. The telegraph line had been strung up the Maine coast as far as Saint John in New Brunswick. Howe could thank the Cunard steamers and New York newspapermen such as Bennett of the *Herald* and Horace Greeley of the *Tribune* for the fact that the line was finally extended to Halifax. The newsmen wanted the overseas dispatches flashed to them as soon as the steamers docked at Halifax. Cunard ships were the speediest carriers of news from Europe.

Earlier, when the telegraph line had been strung from New York to Boston, other New York papers had followed the *Herald's* example and stationed correspondents in Halifax. They boarded the steamers there, went through the overseas journals and prepared their dispatches on the run to Boston; then the race was on to see which paper's representative could beat the others to the telegraph office.

One correspondent outsmarted his rivals by smuggling a crate of pigeons and a case of type aboard the steamers. He printed the headline news on rolls of thin paper. At the entrance to Massachusetts Bay the pigeons were released, each one carrying a capsule dispatch to its home loft in Boston. Cunard himself put an end to that. He gave orders that no pigeons were to be allowed on the steamers.

When Cunard ships began running to New York in 1848, the *Herald* and the *Tribune* employed small fast cutters that picked up the dispatches off Sandy Hook and scuttled back to port with them ahead of the steamer. For about a year the *Newsboy* and the *Cherokee* provided some exciting races up New York Bay into the East River.

But when the telegraph reached Saint John, new tactics were employed. The newspapers had by his time joined together and formed the Associated Press, which had special news packets made up in England. When the steamers reached Halifax, the packets were rushed across the province by pony express to Annapolis, where a coaster was waiting with steam up, ready to speed across the Bay of Fundy to Saint John and the telegraph. No matter what time of the day or night the Cunard steamer passed Sambro Light, a boat was waiting to pick up the news packets, and a rider was waiting on shore, ready for the crosscountry dash. Horses were changed every twelve miles, riders at the halfway point of seventy miles. The fastest horses could make the 140-mile run in eight hours. Stories were told about the speed and stamina of both horses and riders. One black night a rider felt his mount give a "tremendous leap," and did not know until the next day that he had cleared a twenty-foot gap in a washed-out bridge.

The pony express ran for nine months, until the telegraph reached Halifax.

When the new Cunard schedule started in 1848, Halifax had the best overseas communication in America with two steamers a week, one coming and one going alternately to Boston and New York. In addition, Cunard had extended the Halifax–Bermuda packet service to the West Indies and had replaced the sailing packets with steamers. They ran once a month, bringing passengers bound for Europe up from the islands and from South America to connect with the Atlantic steamers.

Halifax had now become, as the visionaries had dreamed twenty-five years earlier, the hub of Atlantic steam trade, with spokes radiating to England, America and the West Indies, and an important telegraph terminal as well. But something was wrong. It had not become a great ocean terminal. Very little cargo was put ashore at Halifax because there was no way to reship it except by sea. Joseph Howe took up the campaign for a railroad to the interior.

The opening of Cunard's New York service marked the turning point in the conquest of steam over sail on the Atlantic. From then on the grand old sailing packets with their elegantly appointed cabins dropped out of the race, one by one. The new steamers, *America, Niagara, Europa* and *Canada,* brought the Cunard fleet up to nine ships. Constantly churning back and forth between England and America—still following the "great circle" route both coming and going, but now running south of Ireland instead of north, past Cape Clear and the new Fastnet Light —these nine steamers were the only ones on the western ocean. Sam Cunard was the undisputed king of the Atlantic. In less than ten years he had brought about a revolution in ocean transportation.

Then, in the middle of that triumphant year 1848, Joe's empire toppled and almost pulled Sam down with it.

Since the slump of 1842, Joe had surged recklessly ahead, expanding his empire each year. He exported huge quantities of fish and timber. His four shipyards turned out from fifteen to twenty vessels a year, most of them under contract to British owners. A typical product of the Cunard shipyards was the *Beraza,* built for the packet service between Liverpool and Mexico. The *Sword Fish,* another packet, made the fastest sailing voyage on record from Liverpool to Pernambuco: twenty-five days, and she was becalmed for three of them.

Joe grabbed at life like a highwayman, trampling on

his enemies. He was a leader in local politics for twenty years. Election day in the towns along the Miramichi often began and ended with rough-and-tumble battles between Cunard supporters and the "fighting men" of the opposing candidate. They fought with clubs and rocks and thumbs in the eye—rowdy lumberjacks from the woods, riggers and caulkers and shipsmiths from the yards. Cunard's men would do anything for him.

Joe had come safely through the panic year of 1847, when fifty business firms in Liverpool went bankrupt, banks closed, and the bottom fell out of the timber market. The following spring, when he returned home from England, he had orders for more ships and seemed as confident as ever. But he had left his wife and children behind in Liverpool, and people wondered, afterwards, if he had known there was trouble ahead.

One day when the packet arrived with the English mail there was a letter from Joe's creditors. Joe shut himself up in his office and sent for his lawyer. A short time later the bank was padlocked, the company store shut down and word spread through the mills and shipyards that Cunard's empire had collapsed. With it, Joe's image as a hero collapsed, too. The workers left their jobs and surged through the streets, forming an angry mob outside his office.

Then Joe appeared, "booted and spurred," according to one observer, and mounted his horse. He rode through the crowd, his big horse shouldering the men aside until they stopped him. Armed with rocks and clubs, they waited for Joe to make the first move. He called to a boy in the crowd to run home and bring his father's pistols. The boy raced off. Joe sat erect in his saddle, staring defiantly at the mob until the boy returned and handed up two pistols. Then he stuck a gun into the top of each high boot and spurred his horse forward. The men scattered, and he rode home.

That night Joe rode forty miles through the woods to a town along the coast where he took a ship for England, leaving his lawyer behind to do what he could with the wreck of his business. He never saw the Miramichi again.

His town of Chatham was ruined. The sawmill and the gristmill, the brickworks, the fish-packing plant, the company store, all shut down. Lumbering and shipbuilding stopped. The workers began to pack up and leave, some by ship, others walking over the forest trails to New England.

Sam was in London. News of the crash reached him two weeks later, and the voyage home took another two weeks. He arrived in Halifax to find that S. Cunard & Co. was in danger of being swept away, too. Since he was his brother's partner in a number of Joseph Cunard & Company's numerous subsidiaries, Joe's creditors had swooped down, demanding payment. Edward had come up from New York, but he and William found themselves unable to cope with the situation. They had locked the company's warehouses and closed up the offices, while lawyers, accountants and staff worked frantically, trying to determine how many branches of the business had tumbled into ruin with Joe.

Within an hour of his arrival on the *Cambria*, Sam had opened up the offices and warehouses and had issued a statement: every one of Joe's creditors would be paid in full. Then he set about finding the money. The demonstration of confidence in his own ability and integrity was overwhelming. Bankers and merchants of Boston as well as Halifax came forward to offer assistance. In two weeks he had secured enough long-term loans to cover Joe's debts.

It took months to get Joe's affairs into some sort of order. There were mountains of papers to go through, as accountants tried to unravel the complicated tangle of Joe's business dealings. By juggling figures, by taking enormous risks and trusting that his luck would hold, he had skated boldly on the edge of bankruptcy for years. Whether Joe himself had realized that his luck was running out at last was a question nobody could answer. But it almost seemed as if, knowing the crash to be inevitable, he had decided it had better be on a grand scale.

Joe went to Liverpool, where he had no trouble finding a job in the office of a ship broker he had previously done business with. He worked hard, lived quietly and waited for the fuss to subside, confidently expecting that all would be forgiven. He gave no thought, apparently, to the people he had abandoned to hunger and despair. Sam sent contributions to the Chatham Relief Fund, knowing that a handout of money did very little to atone for Joe's irresponsible behavior. He was thankful that business failures in the colonies were not of sufficient interest to get into the London papers, so that few of his friends there heard about the Miramichi scandal.

Three years later he advanced Joe enough money to set up his own office in Liverpool. In partnership with a friend, Joe started a firm called Cunard, Wilson & Company, "Ship Valuers and Brokers for the Sale of Ships and Steamers."

The two brothers met often in Liverpool, where they had mutual friends. But Sam stubbornly resisted Joe's efforts to get back on the old companionable footing. No one in the family could forget that Joe had disgraced the good name of Cunard.

# 9

Cunard's complete monopoly of steamer trade between England and America lasted exactly one year. Early in 1849, the first American-built Atlantic steamers appeared. The owner of the Dramatic Line of sailing packets, Mr. E. K. Collins, had obtained a fat United States government contract to carry the mails from New York to Liverpool. One of the conditions of his contract was that his steamers must be faster than those of the Cunard Line.

Collins built four side-wheelers at a cost of $700,000 each. They were the last word in speed and luxury. The steam-heated public rooms had thick flowered carpets, crimson velvet sofas, brocade hangings and handsome spittoons shaped like seashells, "something not found on English ships, as only the Americans engaged in the practice of spitting." The Collins ships had another unheard-of luxury item: "a bath room, with an apparatus for pumping up salt water from the Atlantic."

In 1850, two more companies began running steamers between America and Europe. The New York and Havre Line folded after two of their vessels were wrecked, the *Humboldt* off Halifax and the *Franklin* near Long Island. The Inman Line fared better, operating out of Liverpool for thirty-six years before it was purchased by the American Red Star Line.

Inman steamers were the first on the Atlantic to carry steerage passengers. Before that, the sailing packets had monopolized the profitable immigrant trade. On every home voyage the American packets and those of the Allen Line running between Quebec and Greenock transported settlers to the New World, many "in the lowest depths of destitution, having neither food nor clothing."

On the best of the sailing packets, living conditions were tolerable for the steerage passengers. On the worst, they endured weeks of misery. In the airless holds that had carried cargo to Europe, bunks were set up in tiers. Here the immigrants ate, slept and lived. During storms, when the hatches were battened down, the smell of terror and seasickness was unbearable. Contagious diseases such as typhoid and cholera were common. Unscrupulous captains often packed in more steerage passengers than the law allowed, expecting a certain number to die. If not enough died on the voyage, the surplus passengers were dumped off at some bleak spot on the coast of Newfoundland, where only a few survived.

In the autumn of 1850, the year the Inman Line started, Joseph Howe went to England. Since one of his missions was to attract settlers to Nova Scotia—the other was to try to get money for the railroad—he urged Cunard to build steamers especially designed for the immigrant trade, "ocean omnibuses" that would provide cheap comfortable

A screw-propelled ship of Cunard's Mediterranean fleet, in 1851.

transportation for working-class people. Two years later the Cunard Line launched the *Andes* and the *Alps,* iron ships designed to carry steerage and second-class passengers as well as cabin class. Equipped with the new screw propellers, which left more room for passengers amidships, these two steamers, and the *Etna* and *Jura* which followed a few years later, carried thousands of emigrants to America in comparative comfort and dignity after the horrors of the sailing packets.

In the meantime, the Cunard Company had opened an agency in Paris and had steamers running between Havre and Liverpool to connect with the transatlantic service. Other auxiliary steamers were in service between Liverpool and Glasgow and Liverpool and Belfast. A Mediterranean fleet of six mail steamers, operated by a Cunard subsidiary called the British and Foreign Steam Navigation Company, ran to Gibraltar and the Mediterranean ports, stopped at Malta, went up the Adriatic to Trieste, back to Syria and Turkey and through the Bosporus to the Black Sea. From Liverpool, this voyage took eight weeks and cost £40.

Cunard was chiefly responsible for the organization and supervision of the company's system of liners and coasters. He was the one who handled all the negotiations with the Admiralty and the Treasury regarding mail contracts. Every Cunard employee knew that the final decision about any company policy was made by Sam Cunard, never by Burns or MacIver. He traveled regularly from London to Paris and Liverpool, to New York, Boston and Halifax; and he usually knew what was going on in all those places at any one time.

He always scheduled his Halifax visits for summer, when the weather was at its best. But he had no time any more to sail around the outports, except for quick runs up to the mines at Sydney and Pictou, usually in the company of G.M.A. directors who had come from England. Only one branch of S. Cunard & Co. had been discontinued since the steamship line started. The *Rose,* which came home from the Pacific in 1846 with a full cargo, had been the last Cunard whaler. Sam's old dream of building up a whaling fleet in Nova Scotia had never really got off the ground.

He wrote letters endlessly, wherever he was. Too impatient to dictate to a clerk, he penned much of his correspondence himself in a strong angular hand. He kept in touch with his partners, his agents, the ships' captains, government officials, coal dealers—and managed to keep up a flow of newsy letters to his sons and daughters as well.

Though Isabel and Elizabeth still lived in Halifax with

Mrs. Duffus, he had finally taken a house in Kensington, where he entertained his friends at small, well-planned dinner parties. "The Tennants live quite close by," he wrote to his daughters soon after he moved to Queen's Gate Gardens, "and I have an occasional gossip with them. I shall have them here occasionally and take them to the Opera, etc." Sir Edward Tennant was a former government official who had been stationed at Halifax.

He described a levee at St. James's Palace where "about 200 gentlemen were presented to the Queen," who wore a train of red velvet and a diadem of opals and pearls. He sent messages to his grandchildren. "Tell Maggie I will send a doll for her and also one for little Gwladys and something for Charlie and I hope they will all be good children and learn their lessons and attend to all you say to them," he said in a letter to Jane. Major Francklyn, Jane and their children were in Ceylon, the 37th Regiment having been sent there to put down the series of minor revolts which occurred in 1848.

"Isabel has asked my consent to her union with Mr. Holden," he wrote in the spring of 1850. "He appears to be a very respectable young man, but he has not much money. I must do the best I can for them." Each of his daughters received a yearly allowance of £300, but "if you require a further amount from any unforseen circumstances let me know and you shall have it," he told them. There were many "unforseen circumstances," for none of his daughters married rich men. Sending them money was one way of making up for all the time he had spent away from home when they were growing up. Isabel married Henry Holden in the autumn of 1850 and went to live in Nottingham, not far from Margaret's home.

In New York, Ned and his wife, Mary, a daughter of

the Wall Street financier Bache McEvers, lived in a tall
Fifth Avenue brownstone, number 124, in the fashionable
district north of Fourteenth Street. Mr. Edward Cunard
of the Cunard Steamship Line was a person of some importance in New York. Ned joined the St. George's Society, became very British and proudly introduced his
famous father to such well-known New Yorkers as August
Belmont, William Astor, Judge Pierrepont, Benjamin and
Cyrus Field and Peter Cooper.

Edward had captured an heiress, but William's marriage to Judge Haliburton's daughter Laura pleased the
family more. The Haliburtons were such good old friends.
Willie and Laura had played together as children. Later,
Laura had spent some years abroad, studying art in Paris
and spending the holidays with her mother's people in
England. She was twenty-seven, a year older than Willie.
They were married in December, 1851. Judge Haliburton,
who had once hoped that his artistic third daughter would
capture an English peer and was later secretly alarmed
because she had turned down so many ordinary suitors,
went thankfully off to England after the wedding with
his latest manuscript, *Traits of American Humour*, under
his arm.

Cunard turned over his house on Brunswick Street to
the young couple and hurried back to England to carry
out certain plans of his own. It had been decided that
Jane's oldest children, Maggie, Charlie and Gwladys (always spelled with a *w* in the Welsh manner), should be
sent up from Colombo to live with their grandfather, since
school facilities for children of army officers in Ceylon
were unsatisfactory, and governesses difficult to find.

The children were making the six-week voyage from
Colombo to London on the mail steamer *Narcissus*. Cu-

Bush Hill House as it appears today, much altered since 1860. Probably the two wings at right—one in front and one at the end—have been added since that date. The house is still standing, though the park has been built over.

nard made elaborate preparations for their arrival. The house in Queen's Gate Gardens would not do for them, he decided; they must have a real garden, and ponies to ride. He took a ten-year lease on a country place in Edmonton—Bush Hill House on the Old North Road overlooking the Lea Valley, eight miles north of London Bridge. Bush Hill, owned by the Currie family of bankers, was described as "a capital family residence in the old style, with beautifully timbered grounds and park, entrance lodges, stabling, outbuildings, gardens and appurtenances together about 74 acres."

The great spreading house at Bush Hill became a second home for numerous children over the next ten years. Jane's children—she had nine altogether—came one by one as they reached the age of learning and were joined during the holidays by various cousins. "I shall have so many grandchildren soon that I will not be able to remember them all," Cunard said proudly in 1850, when there were only twelve. By 1860, the number had increased to thirty-six, with still more to come.

He was getting along in years, and perhaps beginning to realize that the penalty for success is often loneliness. Like a man given a second chance, he was pathetically eager to stay at home with his grandchildren. He turned details of company business over to younger men, took fewer trips and went less often home to Halifax. The result was that his sons and daughters, seeing him settled at last in what seemed to be a permanent home, began to use Bush Hill as a family gathering place. Mary, who lived in New Brunswick, Ann, whose husband's regiment had been returned to Halifax for a five-year term, Elizabeth, Willie and Laura, Ned and Mary—they all crossed and recrossed on the steamers for reunions at Bush Hill, where all the little cousins—a dozen, two dozen at a time—were spoiled and petted and showered with gifts by their grandfather. Margaret and Isabel brought their growing families down from the Midlands.

Years later, when they were grown up and married and had children of their own, Cunard's grandchildren recalled those days at Bush Hill with the same nostalgia as their ancestors had talked about the golden age of the duke's time. They remembered being invited, as a special treat, into the great glasshouses where grapes hung on trellised vines and lemon trees flourished, while their grandfather cut the grapes with a pair of nippers he carried on a chain. Often, after breakfast, he would stand at the hall window, an erect white-haired figure in a black tailcoat, waiting for his coachman, who was considered late if he did not arrive some minutes ahead of time. Or he would send a servant running down the hill to see why the special letterbag containing the Bush Hill mail was ten minutes late.

He had never got over his old habit of rising at dawn. When he first moved to Bush Hill and learned that the morning mail was not delivered until eleven o'clock, he did not waste time complaining to the local post office, but went straight to his friend the postmaster general. The delivery system was speedily revised, and from then on Cunard's letterbag arrived every morning at nine.

There were ponies at Bush Hill and a great park for the children to ride in and a garden containing a mysterious round earthwork that was supposed to have been a Roman camp. The children were taken to the village and shown the famous Bell Inn where the hero of William Cowper's poem "John Gilpin" had stopped. On Sundays, they went in a group to the ancient church, and on weekdays the older ones were allowed to make rubbings of the brasses. After Grandmother Duffus died—of old age, at eighty-six—Elizabeth joined her nieces and nephews at Bush Hill.

Judge Haliburton stopped there whenever he was in London seeing his publisher. It was the sort of place he longed to own himself but could not afford. In 1856, however, Haliburton married a wealthy widow, a Mrs. Williams, "well-connected socially," and his dream of living a life of ease and luxury in England came true. Mrs. Haliburton rented Gordon House at Isleworth on the Thames near Twickenham, a mansion built by George I for one of his mistresses. Cunard visited Gordon House, where he found Haliburton looking the picture of a successful author, in a richly furnished library with high

French windows opening into a garden with fountains and clipped hedges.

During those years at Bush Hill, the famous ocean races between the Cunard ships and those of the Collins Line were the talk of England and America, though in fact Cunard and his partners steadfastly refused to compete for the mythical blue riband of the Atlantic (which never existed in material form until well on into the next century). Their captains were issued strict orders never to put speed ahead of safety. Cunard, in particular, was adamant on this point. He had seen too many wrecks—including *La Tribune* long ago—and too many narrow escapes.

In spite of all the precautions taken, the *Europa* had run down and sunk two sailing vessels, the immigrant brig *Charles Bartlett* and the schooner *Florence*. Both had been running without lights.

The *Hibernia* had almost come to grief in the uncertain currents off Newfoundland some years earlier. She had been steaming along in thick fog, unaware that the current had pulled her twenty miles off course, when the rocks of Cape Race loomed ahead suddenly. The engines were reversed and the ship swung clear, with so little room to spare that her port side grazed the cliff. Cunard's little mail steamers *Falcon* and *Kestrel,* running between St. John's and Halifax, and the Inman liner *City of Philadelphia* had not been so lucky. All three were wrecked near the same spot.

Cape Race at the western end of the great circle and Cape Clear on the eastern end were the two main hazards to Atlantic shipping. The *America* had been saved from foundering on the Fastnet Rocks off Cape Clear by her captain's refusal to steam blindly past the danger spot in thick fog. Captain Shannon, who had commanded the *Columbia*, may have been reminded of the night that ship was wrecked on Seal Island. He ordered the engines stopped. Just in time, as it turned out. The *America* drifted over a submerged rock and grounded. Three hours later the tide rose high enough to float her off with no damage. If she had been running at full speed, the results might have been tragic.

The Collins Line, compelled by the terms of their contract to maintain the fastest ships on the Atlantic, ordered full steam ahead through storm and fog. Soon they cut the time from New York to Liverpool to nine and a half days. They got the bulk of the passenger trade because they offered what people wanted, speed and elegance. The Cunard steamers were considered by many to be too conservative. The Cunard Line did put steam heat in the *Arabia* and upholstered the sofas in crimson velvet, but even that up-to-date ship had "no bath room or smoking room, no piano, and only an apology for a ladies' cabin." Passengers who wanted to smoke could sit on camp stools under a canvas shelter on deck. No change had been made in the dining service since the *Britannia* was launched. The same menu was still in use, featuring the same stewed prunes and rice puddings.

But what the passengers enjoying the bathrooms and pianos on the Collins ships did not know was that the engines under them were being forced to the limit of their endurance, and that after every voyage costly repairs had to be made, and burnt-out parts replaced. It was estimated that at the end of six years, repairs to the Collins steamers amounted to more than their original cost. In spite of its popularity, the line was losing money, while the Cunard Line showed a profit.

Cunard's contract with the Admiralty specified that if

Britain went to war, the government could requisition any of the mail steamers for use as carriers. In 1854, when England was sending troops to the Crimea, Cunard did not wait for the government's official demand. He ordered fourteen ships, including eight Atlantic liners, to be converted into warships. In late January, two months before Britain declared war on Russia, the *Niagara* arrived in Liverpool from Boston. Within a week she was on her way to Malta with more than seven hundred officers and men. The *Cambria,* arriving from New York around the same time, was ready for service in four days. The steam-heated *Arabia,* fitted up as a cavalry transport, carried the horses of the Light Brigade to Balaclava, two hundred at a time, suspended in canvas slings. The *Andes* and the *Alps*—which were not mail steamers and so not subject to requisition—transported the wounded from Balaclava across the Black Sea to the hospital at Scutari, where Florence Nightingale and her little band of nurses were working. The *Europa* and two more steamers built for the immigrant trade were used as troopships.

With Cunard's reduced Atlantic fleet barely able to keep up the New York and Boston service, the Collins people were in a position to carry out their threat to "sweep the Cunarders off the ocean." They might have succeeded if the reckless speed of the Collins ships had not resulted in two disasters.

In September, 1854, the *Arctic* collided with the small French steamer *Vesta* off Cape Race and went down with 322 people, including Collins' wife and two children. A year and a half later the *Pacific* sailed from Liverpool and was never heard of again. What happened to her remained a mystery, but it was assumed she had struck an iceberg. These two disasters, plus the loss of their mail contract, ruined the Collins Line, which went out of business in 1858.

The Cunard Line's contribution to the war effort was the subject of a special report in the House of Commons. As usual, the long name of the steamship company was not mentioned. The report identified the ships which had done so much to win the Crimean War as "Mr. Cunard's ships" and the company that owned them as "Mr. Cunard's company." After the report was read, the prime minister, Lord Palmerston, asked the Christian name of "this Mr. Cunard" whom the members were eulogizing. On being told he was silent for a moment, then said thoughtfully, "Sir Samuel Cunard—yes, it sounds well."

But Palmerston's government was defeated soon after that, and it was March, 1859, before Whitehall published the official announcement: "The Queen has been pleased to direct letters patent to be passed under the Great Seal, granting the dignity of a Baronet of the United Kingdom of Great Britain and Ireland unto Samuel Cunard of Bush Hill. . . ."

The London *Times,* which twenty years earlier had dismissed the idea of navigating the Atlantic by steamer as too impractical to be taken seriously, now paid tribute to the pioneer. "It is to Mr. Cunard, more than to any other man, that we owe the route across the Atlantic, which has so closely connected the two worlds as to leave no room for more complete approximation, save through the agency of electricity itself." This meant the Atlantic telegraph cable. Cyrus Field's first cable, completed in 1858, had been a failure, but plans for laying a new cable were under way.

The newly created baronet's coat of arms showed, fittingly, three anchors and the motto "By perseverance."

The Cunard coat of arms, created in 1859 when Samuel Cunard was made a Baronet of the United Kingdom of Great Britain and Ireland.

The crest was a falcon on a rock, one claw resting on a cinquefoil.

That year, at Robert Napier's request, Sir Samuel agreed to sit for a portrait, which Napier presented to Elizabeth on her thirty-second birthday. "The portrait of my father that you have been so very kind as to present to me has been hung up in the dining room at Bush Hill," Elizabeth wrote. The sideboard under it supported a large bronze falcon with outspread wings, copied from the coat of arms.

Letters of congratulations had poured in to Sir Samuel from both sides of the Atlantic. But there was no letter from George Burns. The partners, who had worked together in harmony for so many years, had had several

Sir Samuel Cunard, from an oil painting done in 1859.

disagreements about company policies. In 1858, the disagreements had developed into an open quarrel over the
question of screw propellers versus paddle wheels.

Down in London, the engineering genius Brunel, who
had designed the *Great Britain,* was building his giant
dream ship *Great Eastern,* almost twice as long as any
steamer afloat. Burns thought this wonder ship would put
all ordinary steamers in the shade, and he wanted to meet
the competition by switching to screw propellers on the
mail boats. The Cunard Line was the only one on the Atlantic still using paddle wheels. The Inman Line, the
Allen Line, which began running steamers in 1854, the
newly formed Hamburg-American and North German
Lloyd—all had adopted the more modern screw propeller.
But the enormous *Great Eastern,* which Cunard considered years ahead of her time, was equipped with both side-
paddles and screw propellers.

The four immigrant ships of the Cunard fleet had screw
propellers, but Cunard held out for the safer-looking paddles on the mail boats because he knew that passengers
preferred them. His policy was never to adopt new ideas
until they had been thoroughly tested by someone else.

Burns clung stubbornly to his view, perhaps determined to prove, for once, that he carried as much weight
as Cunard. Cunard clung just as stubbornly to his view.
Finally defeated, Burns retired from business and built a
house on Wemyss Bay on the Firth of Clyde. His place
in the firm was taken by his sons John and James.

Cunard was right about the *Great Eastern.* She was a
failure from the beginning. Her first Atlantic crossing was
a nightmare. High seas swept away the paddle wheels,
broke the rudder, and knocked over the cowhouse. A cow
fell through a skylight onto the passengers in the saloon.

The vessel rolled and pitched so much that both passengers and crew were terrified, never expecting to reach New York.

After that first voyage nobody would sail on her, and the company that built her went bankrupt. She was put up for auction by Cunard, Wilson & Company of Liverpool. So the name of Joe Cunard was written into the history of merchant shipping as the man who auctioned off the world's most famous steamer, the *Great Eastern.*

# 10

Judge Haliburton was much impressed with the distinction accorded his friend, but thought privately it was a pity more titles were not handed out for literary achievement. The Haliburtons often went to London to share Sir Samuel's box at the opera, and whenever the old judge was in town for the day he had lunch with Cunard at the Conservative Club.

Their talk always turned to the colonies. After his marriage, Haliburton paid only two brief visits to Halifax, but he was still keenly interested in what was going on there, and counted on Cunard, who went home more often, to keep him up to date. They reminisced about the old days in Nova Scotia and mourned the fact that the once-important colony seemed to be standing still while the Canadian provinces were developing at a great rate.

Howe's precious responsible government had not performed any miracles, Haliburton grumbled. No wonder

Britain was indifferent to overseas problems, when "those wretched colonies," as Disraeli called them, were so fond of airing petty grievances. As, for example, in the mid-fifties, when the Cunard Line had lost the Canadian mail.

The Canadian government had inaugurated its own overseas mail service, with ships of the Allen Line running between Quebec and Liverpool. A very small amount of the Canadian mail was still carried by the Cunard steamers, and this had been put ashore at Halifax. Nova Scotia demanded a subsidy for sending it on to Quebec. Another squabble developed, and again Britain was drawn into it, with the result that printed notices had been hung in every post office in England advising that no more mail for Canada would be sent by way of Halifax. Letters would "only be sent through the U. S., or by the Canadian mail packet."

Those who had thought that the ocean steamer would make Halifax one of the great ports of the world, simply because it was closer to Europe than any other port, had long since been disillusioned. Steamer after steamer went by in the sea lanes off Nova Scotia, bound for other ports.

The railroad from Halifax to Quebec was still only a dream. Howe, who had for a time held the paradoxical post of chief commissioner of railways, had obtained from the British government "a large imperial guarantee"—that is, a vague promise that funds for building the railroad would be advanced some time in the future. In the meantime, though Cunard's "ocean omnibuses" carried immigrants across the ocean by the thousands, none got off at Halifax. They all went on to the American ports. Those bound for Canada disembarked at New York.

Haliburton contended that if Howe had spent more time on railroad business and less time fighting the General Mining Association, he might have got better results.

Howe's campaign against G.M.A.'s monopoly of "all the workable coal seams in the province" had begun back in the forties with a series of letters in the *Novascotian* addressed to Cunard—Mr. G.M.A. to everyone at home. Later, Howe carried on the campaign from his lecture platform. "Does any man seriously believe that any company would have monopolized for thirty years the mines and minerals of an entire province, had British America been represented in the imperial parliament?" he demanded, aiming at two birds with one stone. He was still hoping to send an M. P.—himself—from Nova Scotia to the British House of Commons.

Beyond pointing out that G.M.A. paid royalties to the province, Cunard had made little effort to justify the monopoly. He seemed unaware, in fact, that a campaign was going on. Then, in the late fifties, a delegation was sent to London to have it out with G.M.A. The Nova Scotia delegates, primed for a good fight, were rather taken aback when, as soon as they had stated their case, Sam Cunard rose and advised the G.M.A. directors that "the claims of the province were not excessive." The matter was quickly settled. All the coal deposits in Nova Scotia except those being worked by G.M.A. were turned back to the province. With his usual diplomacy, Cunard did not point out that G.M.A. was already working the best coal seams.

Ironically, it was Haliburton, not Howe, who gained a seat in the British House of Commons. Though he represented the Cornwall riding of Launceton, Haliburton might as well have been representing Nova Scotia, for most of his speeches were about colonial problems. He obtained his seat easily enough, through the influence of his friend the Duke of Northumberland, but his parliamentary career was not a success.

Laura Cunard spent the summer of 1859 at Gordon House. She was on hand, with Sir Samuel, to hear her father's maiden speech in the House. It was a great disappointment to both of them. Cunard, remembering how once in the old days the young reporter Joseph Howe had been so carried away by Haliburton's eloquence that he forgot to take notes, "waited for the old orator to make a sensation." But the old judge's address was wandering and ineffectual. His once strong voice, weakened by a throat disorder, was barely audible. He spoke of colonial matters at a time when Britain was thinking of abandoning her North American possessions.

Haliburton kept his seat in the Commons for six years, but scarcely anyone noticed him there, or listened to his speeches.

Britain's interest in her North American possessions picked up suddenly when the American Civil War began. She placed her colonies in a vulnerable position by her undeclared support of the South. Halifax became a base of operations for Confederate blockade-runners, while Union warships prowled offshore. When a Union ship fired on the British mail steamer, *Trent*, off St. Thomas and seized two representatives of the Confederate government who were passengers to England, outright war seemed inevitable.

The *"Trent* Affair" blew over, but many U. S. newspapers urged that now was the time for the United States to seize the whole of North America. The southern states could take Mexico, while the northern states annexed the British colonies. The New York *Herald* suggested that

troops be sent up without delay to "destroy the last ves-
tige of British rule on the American continent."

Those were tense years in Halifax, with the threat of
war in the air, but the merchant shippers profited enor-
mously. It was almost, for a time, like the days before
Waterloo, with British troops everywhere and the fleet
back to wartime strength. "The people of the place have
become rich," Sir Samuel wrote after one voyage home.
S. Cunard & Co. enjoyed a period of such prosperity that
William and Laura bought a tract of land in the suburbs
and built a magnificent home which they called Oaklands.

Set in a great park, with massive gates and a Gothic
lodge, Oaklands was built of Philadelphia brick and native stone, its wrought-iron grilles shipped from Scotland.
Willie imported a herd of prize Alderneys to graze in the
park and some rare plants for his conservatory. Vast
greenhouses sheltered winter strawberries which were exported to Boston on the steamers. William's youngest boy,
Cyril, was born at Oaklands.

William had been appointed *agent consulaire de France*
under the French system of selecting representatives from
among the traders of small ports which had no regular
consulate. He received no money, only prestige, and a
gold *medaille d'honneur* from Napoleon III, but the appointment was good for business. Occasional French diplomats and the officers of any French ship that happened
to be in port were received at Oaklands, and the British
senior officers were invited to meet them. Laura entertained in the grand style. Halifax society, which had gone
sadly downhill since Joseph Howe sent the titled governors back to England, welcomed the return to dignity
and fine manners. The diplomats were delighted to discover that Laura spoke their language fluently and had
trained her cooks in the art of French cuisine.

During the early years of the Civil War, the Francklyns returned from Ceylon. Jane's husband retired from the army with the rank of colonel, and settled his family in the French resort town of Boulogne. The ten-year lease on Bush Hill having run out at the same time, Sir Samuel and Elizabeth moved back to Kensington. Number 26 Prince's Gardens was one of a row of tall stucco-fronted houses built in the decade following the Great Exhibition. The houses formed a quadrangle around the gardens, with French windows opening onto balconies overlooking the formally arranged lawns and shrubs and flower beds.

Sir Samuel retired in 1863, at the age of seventy-six. He gave up reluctantly. He had always kept himself in good shape and had outlived all his brothers except Joe and Henry. But a minor heart attack that year finally convinced him that it was time to step aside and let his sons take charge. Edward replaced his father as the steamship company's senior partner. He continued to make his home in New York, dividing his time between England and America as his father had done.

The Francklyns soon began to talk about leaving Boulogne and moving to Halifax, where they could live more cheaply than anywhere in England or France. They had seven daughters for whom husbands had to be found, and Halifax was full of young unmarried British officers.

"I should think in the society of Halifax you would find a better prospect of the settlement of your daughters than you would in any place on this side of the water," Sir Samuel told Jane. He wrote at once to Willie to be on the lookout for a good house, which he would pay for. Getting the Francklyns settled in Halifax and arranging the future of their two boys was something to look forward to now that he had so much spare time.

By the summer of 1864, when Sir Samuel made his last

voyage home, it had been decided that twenty-year-old Charlie Francklyn would be taken into the steamship company's New York office to work under his uncle Edward, while a place would be found for George, later on, in the Halifax office under William's supervision.

Willie had found just the right home in Halifax for the Francklyns—a substantial white house with a widow's walk and a garden running down to the sea, about half a mile from Oaklands. The Francklyns did not occupy this house until after Sir Samuel's death. He never knew that the move back to Halifax resulted in the "settlement" of at least three of Jane's daughters. Two of the girls married up-and-coming young officers—future generals and admirals—of the garrison and the fleet.

On his last visit to Halifax, Sir Samuel stayed with William and Laura at Oaklands, but he spent a few days at the old house on Brunswick Street, the home he had built for Susan almost fifty years before. The district was becoming less fashionable. One or two of the houses had been converted into shops. From the back windows he could look down, over the roof of the little settler's cottage his father had built, to the waterfront and the busy scene at the docks. As a boy, he had watched the high old three-decker ships of the line coming and going. Now the waterfront was crowded with fast American clippers and steam vessels. The old West India traders with their deep keels and long bowsprits were fast disappearing, too.

Only a few of his contemporaries were still alive, old men who still remembered the glitter and easy money of the days before Waterloo. The old privateer Enos Collins was still active at ninety. His estate, Gorsebrook, was near Oaklands. Collins had six million dollars in the bank

Enos Collins.

and boasted about his cellarful of "rare old wine," but he
could still worry along with the other merchants about
certain changes that threatened Nova Scotia.

The three Atlantic provinces, Nova Scotia, New Brunswick and Prince Edward Island, were talking about unit-
ing to form one stronger colony, better able to resist in-
vasion from the south. A meeting was to be held in
Charlottetown to discuss the terms of union. But the
provinces of Canada had invited themselves to the meeting with the intention of promoting a union of *all* the
North American colonies.

For once, the merchants of Halifax were in complete
agreement with Joseph Howe, who warned that any union
with Canada would be utter folly. But Howe's government was no longer in power. He had been defeated in
the last election and had since been made commissioner
of fisheries, a job that kept him away from Halifax for

months at a time. He was helpless to prevent a move which everyone except the politicians in power believed could bring nothing but ruin to the Atlantic provinces.

To most Nova Scotians, being taken over by the United States did not seem half as disastrous as being reduced to "the degraded position of a servile dependency on Canada," which was what the Canadians had in mind. Their scheme was to set up a central government a thousand miles from the sea, from which, though they knew nothing about maritime matters, they would presume to dictate the government of the ocean provinces. It was unthinkable. But the merchants were confident that the people, who must in the end decide the question, since Howe had won for them the right to choose how their country should be governed, would vote against such a "confederation," as the Canadians called it.

It was well for the merchants' peace of mind that they could not see into the future, for the people were never given a chance to vote. Three years later, while the country boiled with indignation and Joseph Howe's faction fought the move with grim despair, the union was pushed through. Nova Scotia was made a province of the new Dominion of Canada.

At once, Halifax became in fact what the British postmaster general had been calling it for some time—an outport of Canada. The ink was barely dry on the document of confederation when Halifax was dropped as a port of call for the Cunard steamers. The new Canadian government had contracted with the Inman line to deliver the overseas mail to the Atlantic provinces. The *Cuba,* which left Halifax on December 21, 1867, was the last Cunard liner to touch that port in almost fifty years.

Sir Samuel did not live to see any of this. He did not

live long enough to see Joseph Howe, worn out with his efforts and convinced that further opposition was useless, accept the fact of confederation and take office under the hated Canadians. For this Howe was reviled by his followers as a turncoat. Howe died a few years later—"of a broken heart," one of his friends wrote, "so deeply wounded by those who had been his friends and should have judged him as stirred by higher motives than anything personal to himself. They might have trusted him; he saw farther than they did."

Neither Howe nor Cunard lived long enough to see the once-powerful empire of S. Cunard & Co. in Halifax dwindle and contract until all that was left was a retail outlet for domestic coal. One by one the Cunard traders disappeared from the ocean. The last sea-blue pennant with its white star was folded away, to be resurrected years later and hung in a museum. Halifax, once journey's end for ships of all the world, slept away the years.

But these events were far in the future that summer of 1864 when Cunard sat with his aged friend Collins on the terrace at Oaklands, while William's children—Alice, little Willie, Arthur and two-year-old Ernest—played nearby.

William had inherited all the Duffus talent for hospitality. Friends and relatives converged on Oaklands, and if half a dozen of them accepted his last-minute invitation to dinner, Laura was not put out. Sir Samuel was very fond of Laura; she had so much of her father's wit and air of distinction.

Most young ladies of the period were taught to do pale aquarelles of trees and brooks and flower arrangements, but Laura was a serious landscape artist who worked with

Laura Charlotte Haliburton (1824–1910), daughter of Thomas Chandler Haliburton, married William Cunard, second son of the Honorable Mr. Samuel Cunard, on December 30, 1851, at Windsor, Nova Scotia.

oils. Unable to attend the Royal Academy, which at that time did not admit female students, she had studied under private teachers in Paris. She worked every morning in her big bare studio at Oaklands. At forty, she had not given up her youthful dream of seeing one of her landscapes hung in the Royal Academy.

In the years since her marriage, Laura had become very much one of the family. The girls turned to her for advice, as they had once turned to Grandmother Duffus.

Edward's wife, Mary, was quite different. She made Edward happy—he had grown fat and contented since his marriage—but Mary always held herself a little aloof from the family. For an heiress, she had some rather provincial ideas, they thought. Her father-in-law's title did not impress her; titles were not democratic. She had not visited England since the beginning of the Civil War because the British upper classes were hostile to the northern states. And she preferred American schools for her children. But Edward had insisted that Bache, at least, ought to be given a proper English education, because he was the oldest son and would one day inherit the title. So twelve-year-old Bache was at school in England with Isabel's son Harry Holden, who was a year younger. Bache spent the holidays at Prince's Gardens with his grandfather and Elizabeth.

Sir Samuel returned to England on the *Scotia,* the last paddle-wheeler built for the line. He had been forced, at last, to admit that paddle steamers were no longer practical. The two latest ships, the *China* and the *Cuba,* were equipped with screw propellers. They were modern, more streamlined, cheaper to operate, but Cunard thought they lacked the beauty and dignity of the *Scotia* with her black and gold paddle boxes and her gold figurehead.

He must have felt a true "proprietor of the Atlantic Ocean" on that last voyage. Though there were other steamship lines on the ocean, the Cunard Line was the undisputed leader. The Civil War had interrupted Cunard's profitable immigrant service, but it had brought American shipping almost to a standstill. Two-thirds of all U. S. overseas mail was carried by Cunard ships.

He was tired after the long journey home. That autumn his health failed rapidly; he became very thin and old and seemed to shrink in height as well, though the habit of a lifetime made him hold his head erect. In December,

Joseph Cunard, circa 1864.

he was in bed recovering from a severe attack of bronchitis when Willie wrote from Halifax that his little boy Arthur had died "of a fever." That Christmas Bache was sent to Boulogne to spend the holidays with Jane's children, and plans for the usual Christmas party at Prince's Gardens were canceled, on orders from the doctor.

But after Christmas, when word came that Joe had suffered a heart attack, Sir Samuel announced that he was leaving at once for Liverpool. Elizabeth and Dr. Cahill—an old friend—tried to persuade him to postpone the journey until spring. Joe's attack had been a minor one, they pointed out; he was only sixty-five, and would probably live another twenty years. Sir Samuel was determined. He had seen little of Joe in the past fifteen years because he had never quite forgiven Joe for the Miramichi affair. Now he was afraid that Joe would die before he could assure him that he was willing to let bygones be bygones. He ordered his bag packed and would have made the journey, shaky as he was, if a note had not arrived from Joe's wife, Mary, saying that Joe was recovering and that his doctor seemed to think he would be as good as new in another month.

On January 16, Joe dropped dead in his tall house on Upper Parliament Street in Liverpool. He died with a flourish, as he had lived, collapsing dramatically in his red and gold drawing room in the presence of half a dozen friends.

Joe's sudden death was a shock from which Sir Samuel never really recovered. Joe, with his changeable outgoing personality and splendid arrogance, had become one of the leading citizens of Liverpool, "justly esteemed for his good business qualities and uprightness of character." The London *Times* paid tribute to his "genial disposition, invariable courtesy, and goodness of heart." Once he had lived like a feudal lord. When he died, leaving a wife and four children, his entire estate amounted to £14,000. In Halifax, S. Cunard & Co. was patiently, year by year, reducing the bank loan that had paid off his creditors after the Miramichi crash. It would be another six years before that debt was wiped out.

In early April, after another attack of bronchitis, it was obvious that Sir Samuel had not much longer to live, perhaps only a few weeks more, the doctor said. The family began to gather at Prince's Gardens. Edward and William had been there since January.

The last attack came at two o'clock on Sunday morning, April 23. The doctor came and stayed with Sir Samuel all that night and the next day. On Monday he was a little better, and by Tuesday, when Laura arrived from Gordon House where she had spent the weekend with her own ailing father, it began to seem that he might recover.

Sleeping at intervals, he had vivid dreams about people and places he had known long ago. Each time he woke up he was so eager to share these dreams with his family that they let him talk, though the doctor had said it was bad for him, and they did not understand half of what he was telling them. In some dreams he was a boy again, under a canopy of ranked bowsprits at the waterfront, watching the sailors unloading strange cargoes. He dreamed about the August morning almost three-quarters of a century before when the whaling fleet had sailed away for the last time. He seemed to be reliving all his years. He had few unhappy memories and few regrets about the way he had managed his life.

But there was still one blot on his conscience—his quarrel with George Burns. On Friday he asked Ned to write Burns a letter.

"My father just now desired me to send his sincerest wishes for your welfare and all your family," Edward wrote, "and this is the last message, I fear, you will ever receive from him. He thinks himself his hours are numbered. . . . He has within the past week spoken of you in the strongest terms of affection, and referred to years long past. Through all the troubles and vexations which afterwards sprang up, he has never ceased to entertain the same regard for you and Mrs. Burns and John and Jamie."

The letter was sent off, and Cunard dozed peacefully through the afternoon. Once, on waking, he said to those watching by his bed, "I have been dreaming about your dear mother." He died at six o'clock, with both his sons beside him.

The date was April 28, 1865. That day's *Times* contained a brief Reuter's Express dispatch from Washington, dated April 15: President Lincoln had been assassinated. The news had taken two weeks to reach London.

In August, Thomas Chandler Haliburton died at Gordon House and was buried in the little churchyard at Isleworth on the Thames.

# 11

If any single year could be selected to mark the end of the pioneer stage of the transatlantic steamer, 1865, the year of Sir Samuel Cunard's death, would be the one. In that year, when the Civil War ended, when the tramp steamers began their wanderings around the world, soon to replace the famous sailing clippers, when the first workable Atlantic cable was being reeled out from the *Great Eastern*, the Cunard ships were queens of the western ocean. But over the next decade, as a new era of speed and luxury got under way, as other steamship lines appeared on the Atlantic and flourished, the Cunard Line went slowly downhill.

The trouble was that without Sir Samuel's strong leadership nobody seemed to know what to do. Charles Mac-Iver was old and unwell. John and James Burns were inexperienced. Edward Cunard—Sir Edward now that he had inherited the title—lacked his father's diplomacy and his ability to impress his ideas on others. Also, he spent too many months of each year in New York. His wife, Lady Mary, who insisted upon being addressed as plain Mrs. Cunard, died there in 1866.

The packet service had been transferred from the Admiralty back to the postmaster general's department. In 1867, when the existing mail contract ran out and a new one was signed, there was so much competition that the Cunard Line had to accept a drastic reduction in the subsidy. It was then that the postmaster general dropped Halifax from the schedule and reduced the service to Boston. Ten years later the practice of paying a fixed subsidy was discontinued. From then on payment varied according to weight.

In 1869, Sir Edward Cunard died suddenly in New York of a heart attack. All his children, three sons and four daughters, were at school in England, and the only member of his family who was on hand to see his coffin placed in the McEvers vault in Trinity churchyard was his sister Jane's boy, Charlie Francklyn.

Edward's oldest son, Bache, was eighteen. William was handed the responsibility of filling the vacant seat in the Cunard-Burns-MacIver partnership and of administering Edward's estate as well. He turned the management of S. Cunard & Co. in Halifax over to his cousin John Morrow and his nephew George Francklyn, sold Oaklands, moved his family to London, and bought a house on the Cromwell Road.

Though William had acted as the company's agent in Halifax, he knew nothing about running a steamship line. But he had a good mind, a friendly disposition and the ability to get along with people. He did not try to impress others with his ideas, but encouraged them to bring out their own. It was a time when harmony in the partnership was needed, for William arrived on the scene just as Thomas Ismay's White Star Line of steamers appeared on the Atlantic.

Ismay ships surpassed in speed and luxury anything yet seen on the ocean. They were the first of the modern luxury liners, with compound engines, promenade decks, saloons extending the entire width of the ship, even bridal suites. One Ismay ship, the *Bessemer*, had a self-leveling floor in the saloon to counteract the roll of the ship. White Star liners were the first to give up candles for the new wick lamps burning paraffin oil derived from petroleum and the first to abandon the great circle route, setting a different course for eastbound and westbound liners.

The Cunard Line, always conservative, had fallen far behind the times. Their ships were plain and old-fashioned. But their record for safety still held. They had never lost a passenger or a letter. The Inman line had lost four ships. The worst disaster on that line was the disappearance of the *City of Boston* with two hundred passengers. The Hamburg-American liner *Austria* had burned at sea, killing 470 people. One ship of the Guion Line had been wrecked, another damaged in collision and another lost when the *Wyoming* grounded on the sand-bars of Sable Island and was only freed by dumping $100,000 worth of cargo overboard.

The wreck of the White Star liner *Atlantic* in 1873 sent passengers scurrying back to the safe old-fashioned Cunard ships. When the *Atlantic*, bound for New York, ran short of coal, her captain decided to change course and refuel at Halifax. In the middle of the night, when the man on watch thought the ship was "about 48 miles from land," she ran full speed into an offshore rock and went

The Cunard house flag of 1878–1934. On a red background is "a yellow lion rampant guardant wearing imperial crown and bearing globe showing western hemisphere." This flag was adopted when the British and North American Royal Mail Steam Packet Company became The Cunard Steam-Ship Company. Shares of the company's stock were soon to be put on the open market, and to attract English investors, the British lion replaced the cross of St. Andrew as the company's symbol.

down with 545 people. It was the worst shipwreck on the Atlantic to that date.

Gradually, over the next few years, the Cunard company pulled itself out of the doldrums. The Mediterranean branch of the company had always been profitable. In 1874, the popular thirteen-week "circular voyage" through the Mediterranean and Black Seas became the forerunner of the modern cruise. The first-class fare of £70 included maintenance aboard ship at each port of call.

Four years later the Mediterranean and Atlantic fleets amalgamated under the name of The Cunard Steam-Ship Company. It was still a private company, with the Burns,

MacIver and Cunard families each holding a third of the stock. But running a steamship line had become such big business that private ownership was no longer practical. The partners decided to make the company a public one. In order to attract buyers on the London stock exchange, they discarded the old blue house flag with its Scottish cross of St. Andrew, and adopted one that was unmistakably British: a golden lion against a red background, wearing an imperial crown, holding a globe of the world. Shares of Cunard stock went on sale to the public in 1880 and were eagerly snapped up by investors.

The next year the company built the *Servia,* the first steel ship of the line, the first lit throughout with electricity. Electric lighting was the most welcome of all improvements on ocean liners, more welcome even than running water in the cabins, which did not appear until the first decade of the twentieth century. The *Servia,* and the *Aurania,* built in 1883, reestablished the Cunard Line as the premier service between England and America, a position it maintained despite the sinking of the *Oregon* in 1886—the second and last peacetime loss in the line's history.

The *Oregon* was off Fire Island, approaching New York, when the schooner *Charles R. Moss* loomed out of the darkness suddenly, struck the steamer amidships, recoiled and struck again. The schooner, carrying a heavy cargo of coal, punched two twenty-foot holes in the steamer's side. The *Oregon* stayed afloat for ten hours, time enough to transfer all passengers and mail to other ships. She went down in shallow water, the top of her mainmast sticking up to mark the spot.

The sensational twin-screw liners *Campania* and *Lucania,* launched in 1893, were the first Cunard steamers

The *Lusitania,* launched in 1907, and sunk by a German submarine in 1915.

The *Mauretania.* Launched in 1907, she became, in the twenties, a status symbol of the fashionable world when rich American tourists began to invade Europe.

to carry no sails and the first with refrigerating machinery. The little stovepipe smokestacks had disappeared,
too. The new steamers had raked-back funnels "big
enough to drive a stagecoach through."

In 1901, Marconi carried out his experiments in wireless telegraphy aboard the *Lucania,* and two years later
it was possible to publish a daily newspaper at sea from
wireless dispatches. The steam turbine made its appear-
ance in the *Carmania* in 1904. Three years later, the
*Lusitania* and the first *Mauretania,* the biggest, fastest
and most popular ships on the Atlantic, were launched.

The *Lusitania* was sunk by a German submarine in
1915, but the *Mauretania* continued to sail for many
years. In the twenties, when rich American tourists in-
vaded Europe, crossing on the *Mauretania* became a
status symbol of the fashionable world. Sophisticated travelers regarded her with the same loyalty and sentiment as
travelers in the fifties and sixties regard the *Queen Mary*
and the *Queen Elizabeth.*

The traveler who in 1840 shivered in the unheated cabins of the *Britannia,* dreaming of "the most luxurious of
all enjoyments after a sea voyage—a warm bath," while
the little steamer groaned and shuddered across the Atlantic under a cloud of black smoke, could not have imagined a day when such giants as the queens would cross
from New York to Southampton in less than five days,
each carrying up to four thousand passengers and crew.
Instead of one "saloon" furnished with straight-backed
chairs, today's liners have spacious lounges, elegant res-
taurants, cinemas, swimming pools, dance bands—every
conceivable amenity "laid on," to quote steamship par-
lance. Stabilizers keep the ship steady, radar signals warn
of danger ahead, ship-to-shore radio, telegraph and tele-

phone communication are taken for granted. The clouds of smoke disappeared when oil replaced coal as a fuel.

But even as the famous queens were being built in the thirties, another great revolution in ocean travel was shaping up. Today, with jet planes speeding passengers between New York and London in a matter of hours, the transatlantic steamer is no longer a necessity. But it is still a safe and most pleasant way to travel.

Sir Samuel Cunard left an estate of £350,000 (in dollars, about one and a half million)—not a great fortune, even in those days. In New York, at the same time, Cornelius Vanderbilt was piling up a railroad fortune of 75 million dollars.

Cunard bequeathed £20,000 to each of his daughters, the rest to Edward and William. William was a shrewd investor. Over a period of years he built up his own inheritance, and that of Edward's children, into such considerable fortunes that the boys of the next generation could live as they pleased. Ernest, who succeeded his father as a director of the steamship line, was the only one of William's sons who made a career of business.

Sir Bache Cunard, Edward's son, inherited a sizable fortune from his mother as well. He lived the life of a country gentleman at Nevill Holt, a Georgian castle covering several acres near Market Harborough in Leicester. From a second estate on Grymes Hill, Staten Island, he could watch the Cunard steamers entering New York Bay. American-born Lady Cunard was a famous and witty hostess of the Edwardian era and, in the thirties, a friend and supporter of Edward VIII and Mrs. Simpson. Sir Bache and Lady Maud had one daughter, Nancy. A "flapper" debutante during World War I, Nancy Cunard be-

The *Queen Mary,* shown entering New York harbor for the first time, on her maiden voyage in June, 1936.

The *Queen Elizabeth.* Launched in September, 1938, she made a secret maiden voyage in March, 1940, and was then used for troop transport during World War II. Her first commercial sailing was in October, 1946.

came a leading member of London's postwar literary set, a champion of the surrealist school of painting in Paris and a writer of some repute.

Sir Bache was not fond of society. To fill his days, he took up silversmithing as a hobby. He also had a forge in the castle garden where he did ornamental ironwork and made shoes for his horses. On his death in 1925, his brother Gordon became the baronet. The title went next to Gordon's son Edward, then to William's branch of the family.

The habit of industry was still strong in William's generation. William never wasted a minute of his life. Like his father, he is remembered in family legend as standing with a watch in his hand, expecting someone to be late.

William and Laura occupied a succession of beautiful country houses near London. In 1882, they bought Little Strawberry Hill at Twickenham, near the larger Strawberry Hill with its "Gothic castle" made famous by Horace Walpole. A year later, they moved to Lebanon Park in the same area. Wherever he lived, William had a garden, with glasshouses where he grew exotic fruits. The fruit grown at Lebanon Park was sold at Solomon's, the exclusive market in Piccadilly. Orleans House, the estate adjoining Lebanon Park, purchased from the exiled son of Louis Philippe, duc d'Orleans, was the most magnificent of William's houses. Built in the eighteenth century, the "octagon" with its superb plaster work had been added by the famous architect James Gibbs, a pupil of Wren's.

There was a town house in Eaton Square, too, and a winter home in France. The Villa Lefevre, overlooking the Mediterranean at Montboron near Nice, had a charming old-world garden with rose-covered terraces stepping down to the sea. Laura's studio looked toward the Estérel Mountains. She continued painting throughout her busy life. When she was past seventy, her dream of a lifetime came true. One of her landscapes, "Misty Evening on Richmond Hill," was accepted for the Royal Academy's annual exhibition.

Wherever William and Laura were—at Twickenham, at 95 Eaton Square, at Montboron—other members of the family gathered. Sir Samuel Cunard had, altogether, forty-five grandchildren, though six did not survive childhood. By the end of the century his descendants numbered in the hundreds. William was the grand patriarch of this clan, the one who kept an eye on distant cousins and little grandnephews. He was never happier than when his home resembled an inn, with people coming and going and extra places being set for dinner. A gift-giver like his father, he handed out generous sums of money. Then a thrifty streak inherited from his sober grandfather Abraham would make him say, "Spend it wisely; don't be extravagant."

William remembered old family stories and passed them on to following generations. He told how a bag of gold coins turned up by a settler's plow in Pennsylvania had started the Cunards on the road to fortune, and how a hundred years later they were driven out of Philadelphia into the wilderness and had to begin all over again, and how his grandparents had met on the crowded little ship sailing north from New York. But for him the important years were those of his father's time, when the railroad, the steamboat and the electric telegraph changed the whole pattern of transportation and communication.

William outlived all his sisters. He died in 1906, Laura in 1910. Ernest, who took his father's place on the Cunard

The Cunard–White Star house flag. In 1934 the Cunard line and its old rival, the White Star line, merged to form Cunard–White Star.

board of directors, was the last member of the family to take part in the management of the company. No Cunard has been on the board since Ernest retired in 1922.

But the many descendants of Sir Samuel Cunard, now scattered halfway around the world, still feel a personal pride in the line's record of achievement. To them and to the world the great Cunard ships of today are fitting memorials to the small-town merchant who founded the first and most famous of all steamship lines.

Sir Samuel's contribution to world development was acclaimed by the noted historian of merchant shipping, W. S. Lindsay. If ever the world's benefactors were estimated at their true worth, Lindsay said, the names of Samuel Cunard and his partners would rank among those who, "by their gallant enterprise have made the world richer by giving an unprecedented impetus to commerce, and have rendered inestimable service to the people of every country."

# Bibliography

Albion, Robert Greenhalgh. *Square-Riggers on Schedule*. Princeton: Princeton University Press, 1938.

Babcock, Franklin Lawrence. *Spanning the Atlantic*. New York: Alfred A. Knopf, 1931.

Campbell, Duncan. *History of Nova Scotia*. Halifax, 1873.

Chittick, V. L. O. *Thomas Chandler Haliburton*. New York: Columbia University Press, 1924. (Reissued by AMS Press, New York.)

Dickens, Charles. *American Notes*. London: Chapman & Hall, reprinted 1907. (Reissued by Oxford University Press, New York, and Peter Smith, Gloucester, Mass.)

*Fortunes Made in Business* (anthology). Vol. 2. London: Sampson Low, Marston & Co., 1884.

Fry, H. *History of North Atlantic Steam Navigation*. London: Sampson Low, Marston & Co., 1896.

Haliburton, Thomas Chandler. *An Historical and Statistical Account of Nova Scotia*. Halifax, 1829.

Haliburton, Thomas Chandler. *The Old Judge or Life in a Colony*. London, 1843.

Hodder, E. *Sir George Burns*. London: Hodder & Stoughton, 1892.

Jones, Clement Wakefield. *Pioneer Shipowners.* Liverpool: Journal of Commerce & Shipping Telegraph, 1935.

Lindsay, W. S. *History of Merchant Shipping.* 4 vols. London: Sampson Low, Marston & Co., 1876. (Reissued by AMS Press, New York.)

Maginnis, A. J. *The Atlantic Ferry.* London: Whittaker & Co., 1892.

Napier, James. *Life of Robert Napier.* London: William Blackwood & Sons, 1904.

*Nova Scotia Historical Society Collection.* 34 vols.

Parry, E. *Memoir of Rear Admiral W. E. Parry.* London: Longmans, Green, & Co., 1857.

Rainey, Thomas. *Ocean Steam Navigation and the Ocean Post.* New York, 1858.

Roy, James Alexander. *Joseph Howe.* Toronto: The Macmillan Company, 1935.

# Index

*Acadia,* steamer, 104, 114
*Accommodation,* first Canadian passenger steamer, 41
Albion Coal Mine, 51, 63, 76, 102
Allen Line, 144, 158, 160
*America,* steamer, 139, 152 f.
American Civil War, 163, 171
American Revolution, 12
American sailing packets, 43, 91, 115, 117, 139
Annapolis Mining Company, 55
*Arabia,* steamer, 153 f.
*Arctic,* steamer (wreck of), 154
Associated Press, 138
*Atlantic,* steamer (wreck of), 178 f.
Atlantic telegraph cable, 155

Bennett, James Gordon, 86, 116, 121, 136
Bermuda, postal service, 35 f., 75, 112, 138
Black Ball Line, 43, 115
*Britannia,* steamer, 104 ff., 116 f., 121, 125, 182
British and Foreign Steam Navigation Company, 145
British and North American Royal Mail Steam Packet Company, 98 ff.
*British Queen,* steamer, 82 f., 86 f., 115, 117
Burns, Sir George, 91 f., 98, 131, 146, 156, 158, 174
Burns, James, 158, 174, 176
Burns, John, 158, 174, 176
Bush Hill House, 149 ff.

*Cambria,* steamer, 141, 154
Canada, postal service, 36 f., 90, 112, 118, 125 f., 161

*Cape Breton,* steamer, 73, 76
*Chebucto,* brig, 48, 65, 71
Coal mining; *see* G.M.A.
Collins, Enos, 28, 49, 52, 54, 67, 166, 169
Collins Line, 143 ff., 152 ff.
*Columbia,* steamer, 104, 115, 123 f., 152
*Countess of Harcourt,* tea ship, 58
Crimean War, 154 f.
*Cuba,* steamer, 168
Cunard, A. & Son (formation of), 26
Cunard, Abraham, 12 ff., 20, 23 f., 29, 34, 47 ff., 187
Cunard, Ann (Mrs. Allen), 53, 109, 132
Cunard, Bache, 171 f., 177, 183, 185
Cunard, Edward Sr., 17, 32, 34, 48, 56
Cunard, Edward Jr. (Ned), 46, 54, 63, 65, 105, 119, 131, 147 f., 165, 170 f., 173 f., 176 f.
Cunard, Elizabeth, 63, 106, 132, 146, 151, 156, 165, 172
Cunard, Ernest, 169, 187
Cunard fleet (sailing vessels), 26, 48 f., 61
Cunard, Henry, 17, 24, 32, 34, 47 f., 50, 63, 66, 80, 120, 165
Cunard, Isabel (Mrs. Holden), 63, 106, 132, 146 f., 171
Cunard, Jane (Mrs. Francklyn), 46, 80, 106, 111, 121, 165 f.
Cunard, John, 17, 32, 34, 48, 132
Cunard, Joseph, 17, 32, 34, 50 f., 56, 66, 76 ff., 81, 92, 97 f., 100 ff., 119 f., 128, 139 ff., 159, 165, 172 f.

( 190 )

Cunard, Laura Haliburton, 109, 148, 163 f., 166, 169 f., 173, 185 ff.
Cunard, Margaret (Mrs. Mellish), 46, 80, 106, 132
Cunard, Margaret Murphy, 13, 15 ff., 23 f., 34, 37
Cunard, Mary (Mrs. Parr), 17, 25 f.
Cunard, Mary (Mrs. Peters), 46, 80
Cunard, Robert, 12 f., 18, 32
Cunard, S. & Co. (formation of), 18
Cunard Steam-Ship Company, 179 ff.
Cunard, Susan (Mrs. Ray), 17, 32
Cunard, Susan Duffus, 29, 32 ff., 37, 39, 46, 62
Cunard, Susie, 46, 53, 63
Cunard, Thomas (of Philadelphia), 12
Cunard, Thomas, 17, 32, 34
Cunard, William Sr. (Will), 17, 22, 24, 32, 47
Cunard, William Jr. (Willie), 54, 81, 87, 106, 131, 148, 164 ff., 169, 172 f., 177 f., 183 ff.
Cunard, Wilson & Co., 142, 159
Curacao, steamer, 74
Currency, 30, 54, 61

Dalhousie, Countess of, 37
Dalhousie, 9th Earl of, 39, 47
Dalhousie, 10th Earl of, 78
Dickens, Charles, 85, 116, 121
Disraeli, Benjamin, 79, 161
Douglas, Sir Charles, 31
Duffus family, 29, 31 ff., 45 f., 61, 64, 80, 132
Duffus, Susannah, 32 f., 45 ff., 63 ff., 80, 111, 132, 146, 151

East India Company, 51 ff., 58 f., 76, 79, 94
Edward, Duke of Kent, 20, 60
Enterprise, steamer, 55
Erie Canal, 57, 127
Europa, steamer, 139, 152, 154

Falmouth packets (Royal Mail), 18, 21, 35, 87 f., 91, 100
Field, Cyrus, 148, 155
Francklyn family, 111 f., 147 f., 165 f., 177
Frederick, Duke of York, 53, 60
Fulton, Robert, 41

General Mining Association (G.M.A.), 60 f., 63, 76 f., 102 f., 117 f., 136, 146, 161 f.
Great Britain, steamer, 130, 158
Great Eastern, steamer, 158 f., 176
Great Western, steamer, 82 ff., 89, 91, 100, 115, 117, 130 f.
Greeley, Horace, 136

Haliburton, Laura; see Cunard, Laura
Haliburton, Thomas Chandler, 27 f., 55, 66, 84 ff., 113, 134 ff., 148, 151, 160, 162 f., 175
Halifax Banking Company, 54
Halifax Grammar School, 22, 31
Halifax Whaling Company, 59, 69
Hibernia, steamer, 124, 152
Hill, Sir Rowland, 88
Hooker, Sir William, 122
Howe, Joseph, 56 f., 66, 68 ff., 79, 84 ff., 121, 126 f., 129, 134 ff., 144, 160 ff., 167 ff.

Immigrants, 37, 86, 144 f.
Inman Line, 143, 152, 158, 178
Ismay, Thomas, 178

Lardner, Dr. Dionysius, 82 f.
La Tribune, frigate (wreck of), 21 f., 152
Lawrence, Capt. James, 28
Liberator, steamer, 56
Lighthouses, 21, 49, 71 f.
Lincoln, Abraham, 175
Liverpool, steamer, 82 f., 115, 117
Liverpool Packet, privateer, 28 f.
Longfellow, Henry W., 107
Lusitania, steamer, 182

( 191 )

McDougall, Capt. John, 75
MacIver, Charles, 98, 177
MacIver, David, 98, 100, 131, 146
McKay, Donald, 122
Marconi (wireless telegraphy), 182
*Margaret,* schooner, 25, 33; ship, 61; steamer, 124
*Mary Ann,* brig, 48
*Mauretania,* steamer, 182
Mediterranean fleet (Cunard), 145 ff., 179
Melbourne, Lord, 79
Molson, John, 41
Morrow family, 80, 131
Mount Rundell, 66, 102 f., 121
Murphy family, 13, 16, 26, 63, 80

*Nancy,* schooner, 26
Napier, Robert, 57, 94 ff., 98, 156
Newfoundland postal service, 112, 126, 152
Nightingale, Florence, 154

Ocean Steam Ship Company, 43
*Oregon,* steamer (sinking of), 180

*Pacific,* steamer (loss of), 154
*Pacific,* whaler, 60, 70
Parr, Capt. John, 25 f.
Parry, Sir William Edward, 41, 53, 88 ff., 104, 122, 131
Peninsular War, 25
Pictou Academy, 32, 34
*Pocahontas,* steamer, 73
Pollok, Gilmour & Co., 49
Pony express, 116, 138
Postage stamps, 88
Postal service, general, 18 f., 35 ff., 86, 88, 90, 118
*President,* steamer, 115 ff.
*Prince of Waterloo,* whaler, 44
Privateers, 28 f.
Pyke, Capt. George, 70

Quebec and Halifax Steam Navigation Company, 56

*Rachel,* whaler, 44

Railroad, Halifax to Quebec, 127 ff., 139
Railroads, 73, 76, 90, 116, 125, 127
*Rose,* whaler, 91, 99, 121, 146
Royal Geographical Society, 122
*Royal William,* steamer, 72 ff.
Running lights, 107, 131

St. Laurent, Julie, 20
*Samson,* locomotive, 103
*Samuel Cunard,* whaler, 91
*Savannah,* steamer, 43
*Scotia,* steamer, 171
Seal Island, 71 f., 123 f.
*Servia,* steamer, 180
Shannon, Capt. Neil, 123 f., 153
Shipbuilding, Jos. Cunard & Co., 101, 139
Shubenacadie Canal Company, 57 f.
*Sirius,* steamer, 83 ff., 89
Smith, Richard, 66, 77
*Susan,* brig, 54, 59
*Susan and Sarah,* whaler, 70 f.
*Swiftsure,* steamer, 42
Sydney Coal Mine, 76

Tea imports, 52 ff., 58 f., 76
Telegraph communication, 136
Tennant, Sir Edward, 147
Timber, 49 ff., 77
*Tyrian,* packet, 84 f.

*Unicorn,* steamer, 102, 105 ff., 112, 116, 118, 126
*United Kingdom,* steamer, 57

Victoria, Queen, 60, 68, 84, 116, 134, 147, 155

War of 1812, 27, 35
Waterloo, Battle of, 35
Webster, Daniel, 113
Welland Canal, 57
Western Railroad, 116
Whaling, 19 f., 44 f., 59 f., 69 ff., 91, 98, 146
*White Oak,* ship, 29
White Star Line, 178